Faassen's catnip • Nepeta x faassenii • common lilac • Syringa vulgaris
porphyrophylla "Gerda" • sugar maple • Acer saccharum media
n niponicum • Chicago Hardy fig • Ficus carica • fa
muticum • Chinese silver grass • Miscanthus sinensis • flower
• Hosta plantaginea var. "Grandiflora" • kiss-me-over-the-garden-gate
rangea • Hydrangea quercifolia • white coneflower • Echinacea purpurea
m perfoliatum • black-eyed Susan • Rudbeckia fulgida • swamp sunflower
ybrida "Lucky Charm" • garden speedwell • Veronica longifolia • borage
retail" • wild garlic • Allium vineale • Eastern bottlebrush grass • Elymus
iry alumroot • Heuchera villosa • large-leaved aster • Eurybia macrophylla
us maximiliani • Persian buttercup • Ranunculus asiaticus • tree peony
Syringa vulgaris • garden tulip • Tulipa gesneriana • elderberries "Gerda"
• intermediate wood fern • Dryopteris intermedia • Japanese painted fern
ardy" • false sunflower • Heliopsis helianthoides • blunt mountain mint
nal flower • Lobelia cardinalis • gray-headed coneflower • Ratibida pinnata
den-gate • Persicaria orientalis • blue cohosh • Caulophyllum thalictroides
purpurea var. "Alba" • Mexican sunflower • Tithonia rotundifolia • cu
p sunflower • Helianthus angustifolius • Lucky Charm Japanese anemone
olia • borage • Borago officinalis • mountain fleece "Firetail" • Persicar
grass • Elymus hystrix • scarlet catchfly • Silene regia • Japanese maple
urybia macrophylla • American basswood • Tilia americana • Maximilia
iaticus • tree peony • Paeonia suffruticosa • Faassen's catnip • Nepeta
ana • elderberries "Gerda" • Sambucus nigra f. porphyrophylla "Gerda"
termedia • Japanese painted fern • Anisocampium niponicum • Chi

ardy fig • Ficus carica • Chicago Hardy • false sunflower • Heliopsis
helianthoides • blunt mountain mint • Pycnanthemum muticum • Chines
lver grass • Miscanthus sinensis • cardinal flower • Lobelia cardinalis
ray-headed coneflower • Ratibida pinnata • August lily • Hosta plantagine
var. "Grandiflora" • kiss-me-over-the-garden-gate • Persicaria orientalis
lue cohosh • Caulophyllum thalictroides • oakleaf hydrangea • Hydrange
quercifolia • white coneflower • Echinacea purpurea var. "Alba" • Mexica
nflower • Tithonia rotundifolia • cup plant • Silphium perfoliatum
ack-eyed Susan • Rudbeckia fulgida • swamp sunflower • Helianth
ngustifolius • Lucky Charm Japanese anemone • Anemone x hybri
"Lucky Charm" • garden speedwell • Veronica longifolia • borage • Bora
ficinalis • mountain fleece "Firetail" • Persicaria amplexicaulis "Firetai
wild garlic • Allium vineale • Eastern bottlebrush grass • Elymus hystr
scarlet catchfly • Silene regia • Japanese maple • Acer palmatum • hai
umroot • Heuchera villosa • large-leaved aster • Eurybia macrophylla
merican basswood • Tilia americana • Maximilian sunflower • Helianth
aximiliani • Persian buttercup • Ranunculus asiaticus • tree peony
aeonia suffruticosa • Faassen's catnip • Nepeta x faassenii • common lila
yringa vulgaris • garden tulip • Tulipa gesneriana • elderberries "Gerda
ambucus nigra f. porphyrophylla "Gerda" • sugar maple • Acer sacchari
intermediate wood fern • Dryopteris intermedia • Japanese painted fe
Anisocampium niponicum • Chicago Hardy fig • Ficus carica "Chica
ardy" • false sunflower • Heliopsis helianthoides • blunt mountain mi
Pycnanthemum muticum • Chinese silver grass • Miscanthus sinens

STILL LIFE

With essays by James Baraz, Douglas Tallamy, and W. M. Hunt

JANE FULTON ALT
STILL LIFE

A Photographer's Journey Through Grief and Gardening

ᒪ山

Contents

For Howard

Foreword

I was never a gardener.

Then my husband died, leaving behind an extensive, newly planted native garden. His radical transformation of the green space around our home was stunning. He had worked tirelessly and methodically as he pulled up our lawn and seeded a sanctuary. In the autumn of his life, he had planted a garden for the future.

I asked him one day, "When you are gone, who is going to take care of this garden?" He just looked at me and smiled.

Little did I know it was to be the greatest gift he could have given to me. The garden and the camera have been my loyal and constant companions, a potent combination in adjusting to this new life.

These photographs and thoughts represent the start of my journey.

— Jane Fulton Alt

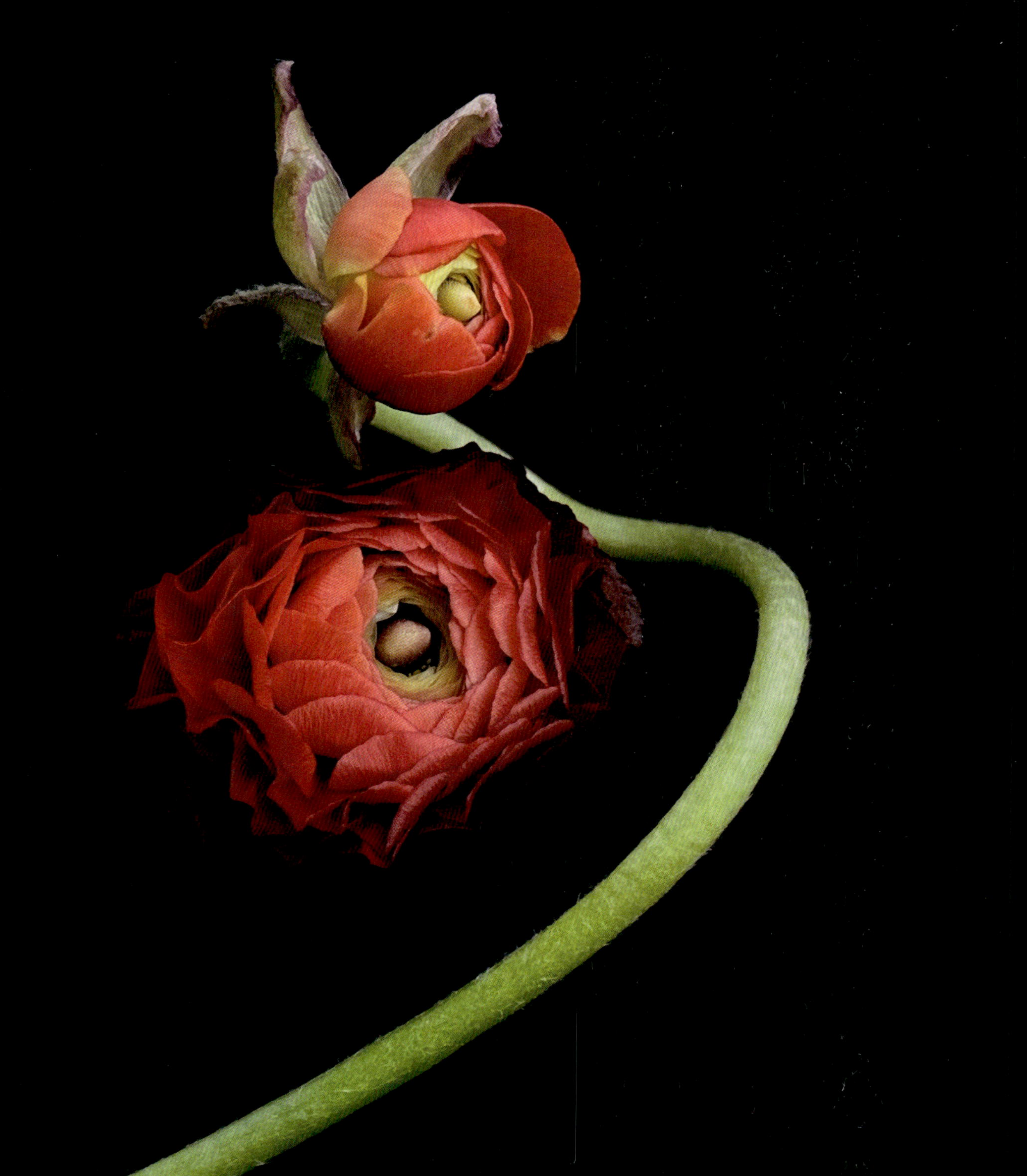

Flowers offer a pathway for mending a broken heart.

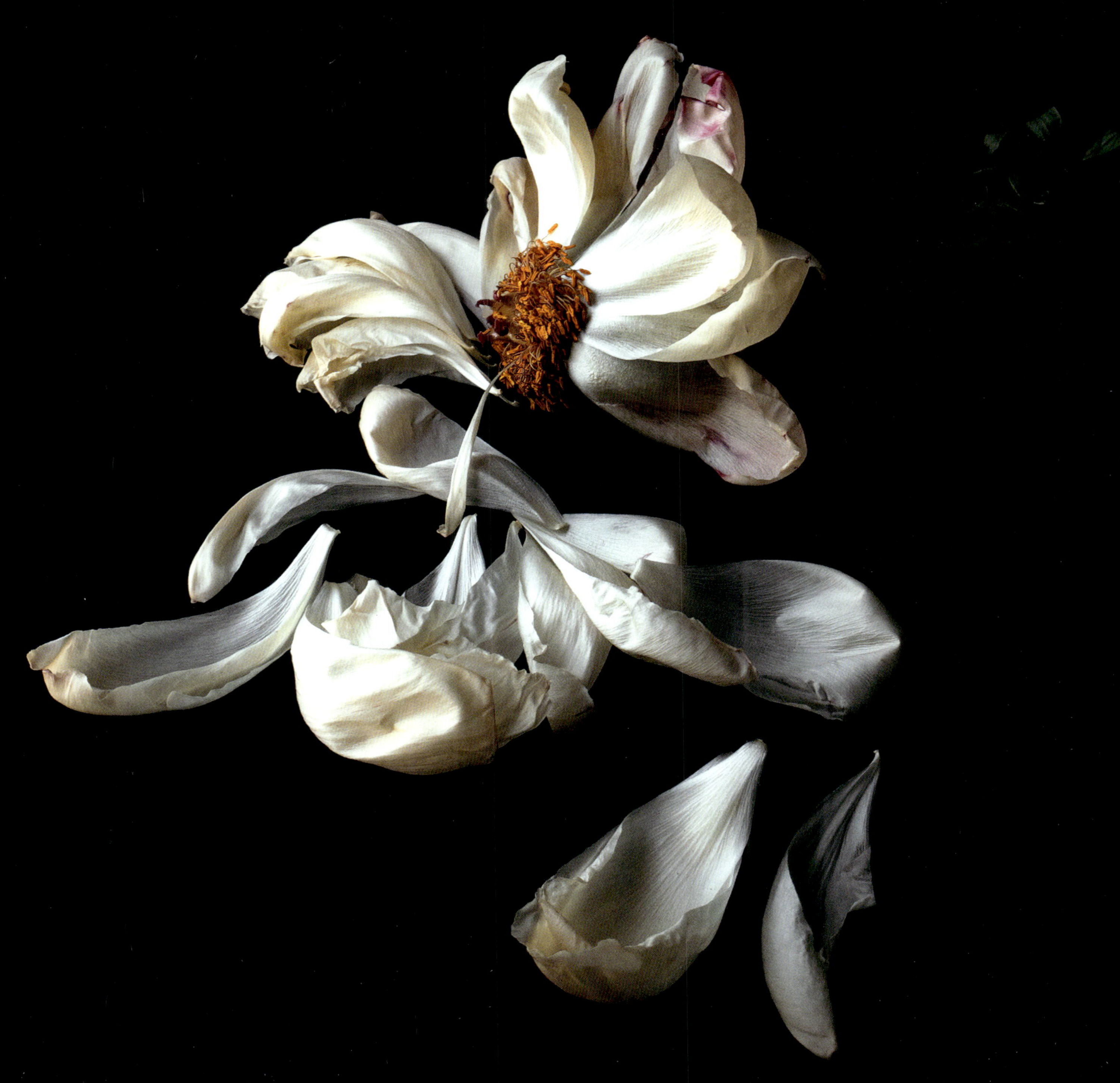

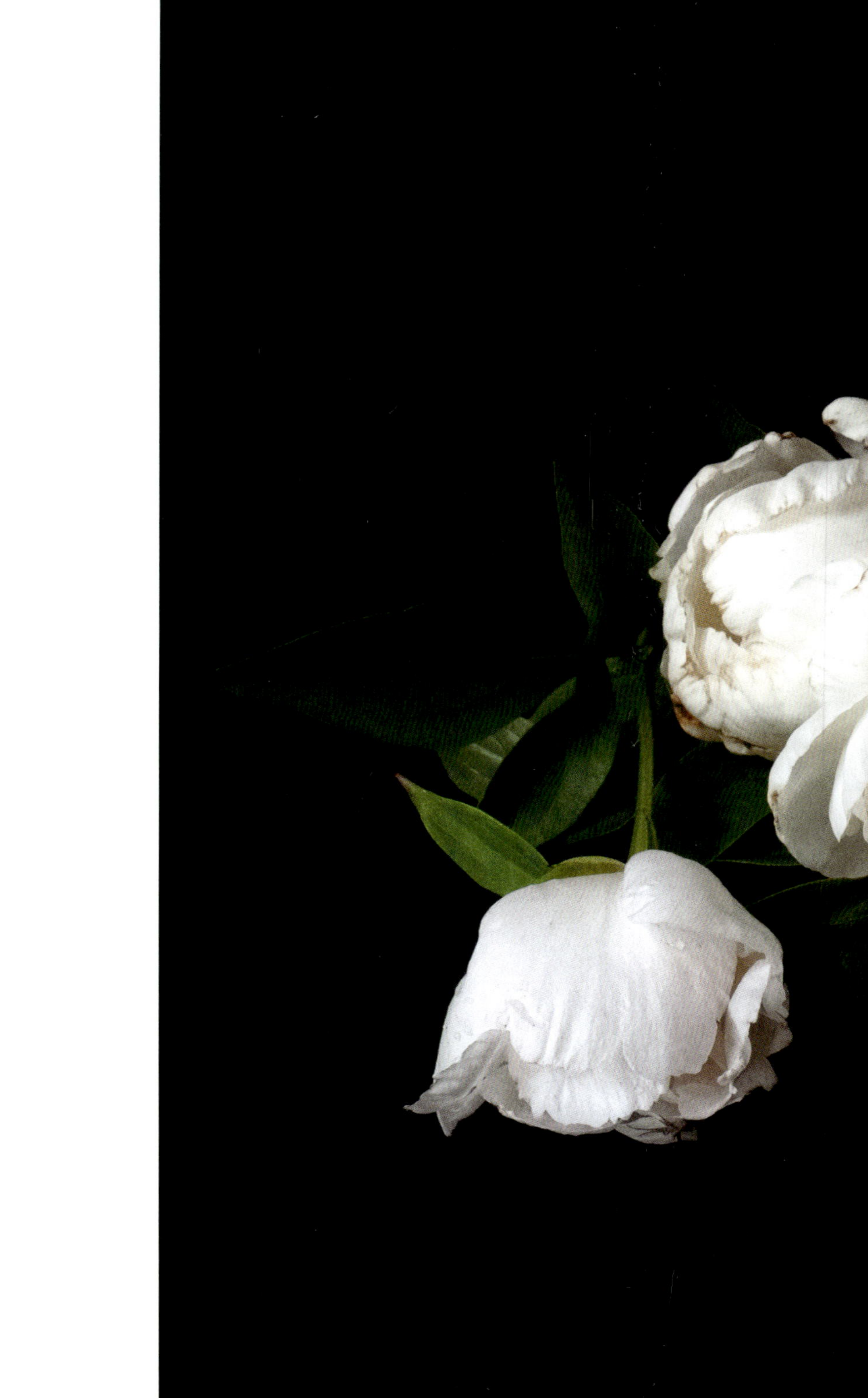

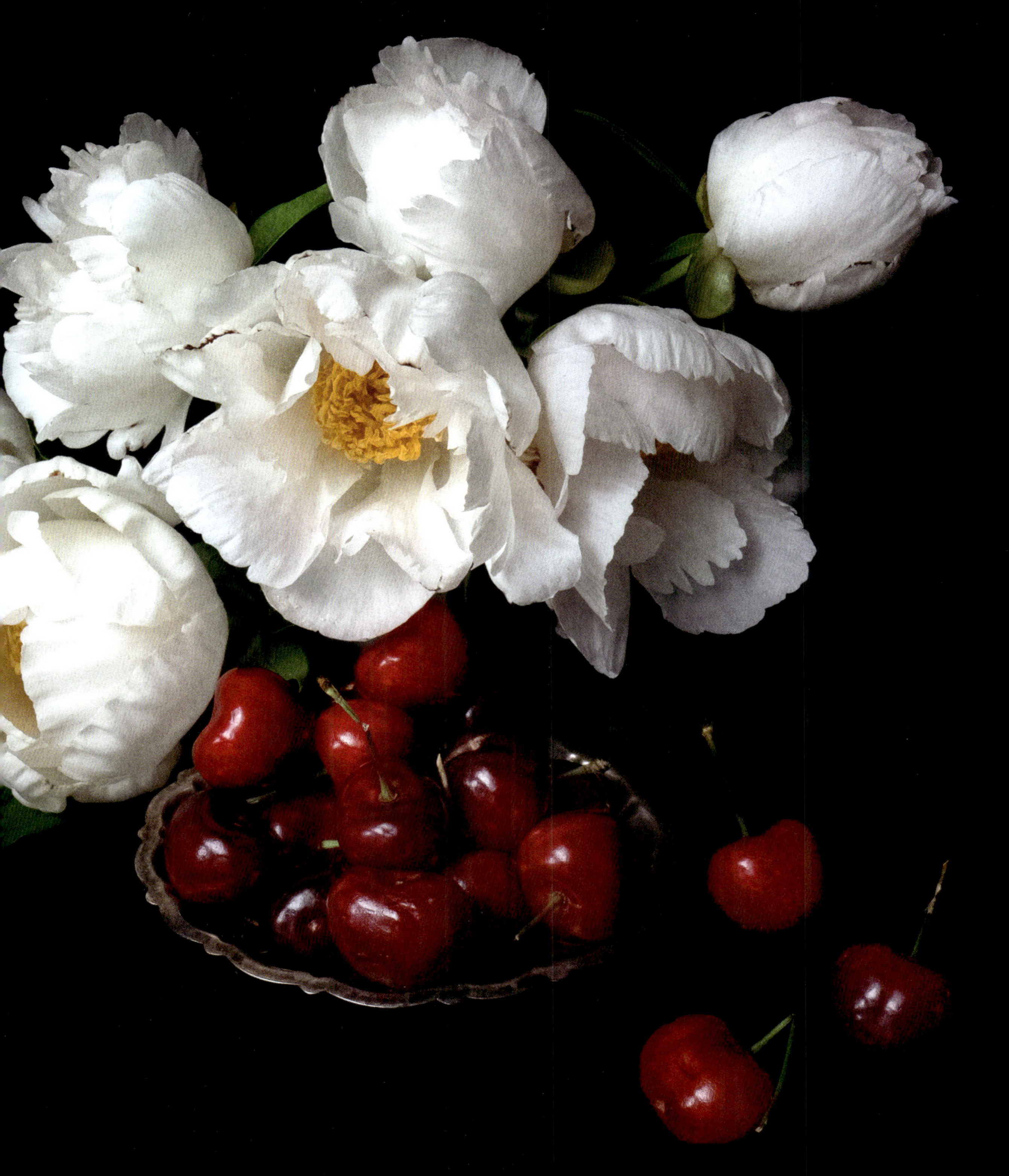

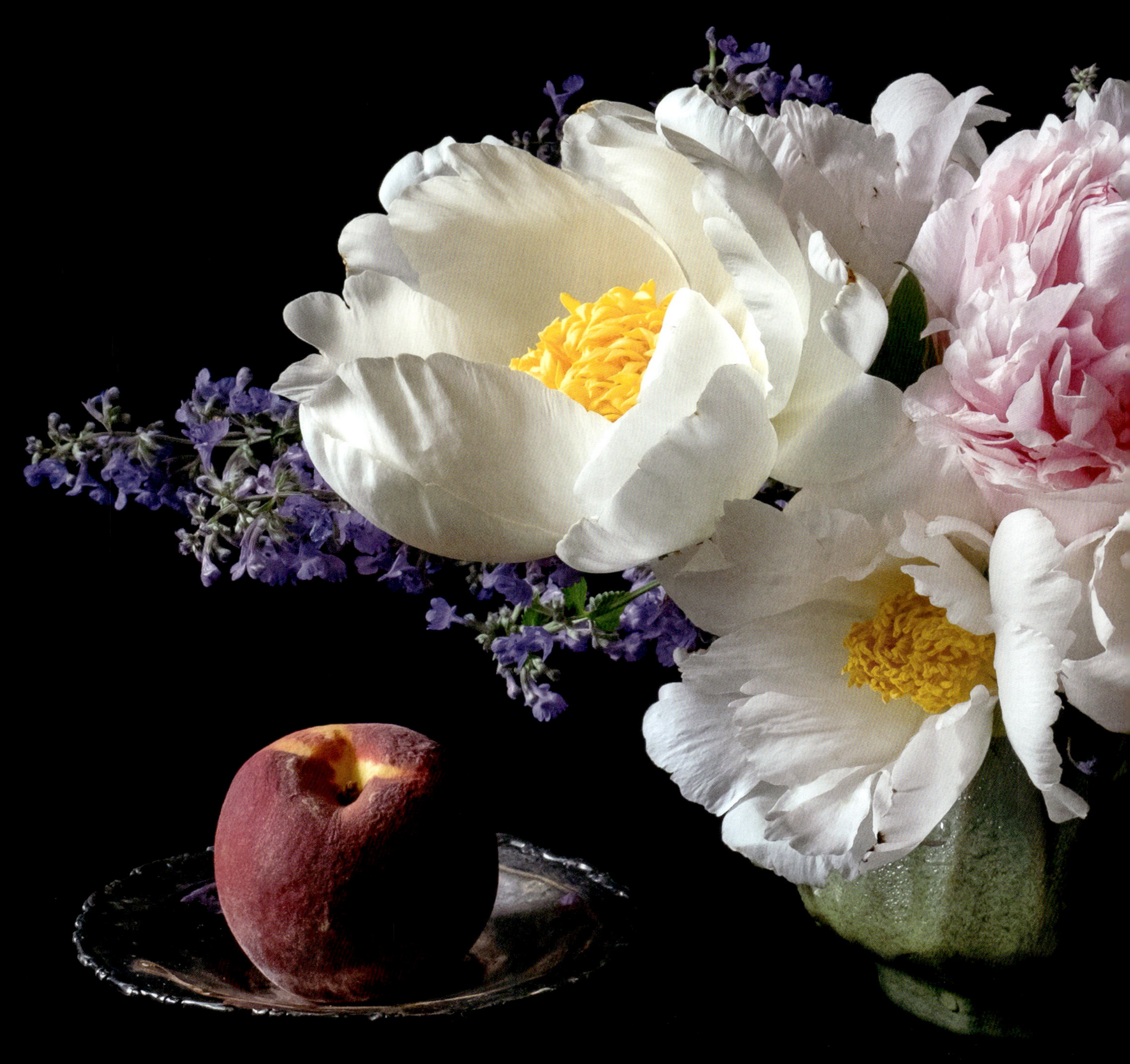

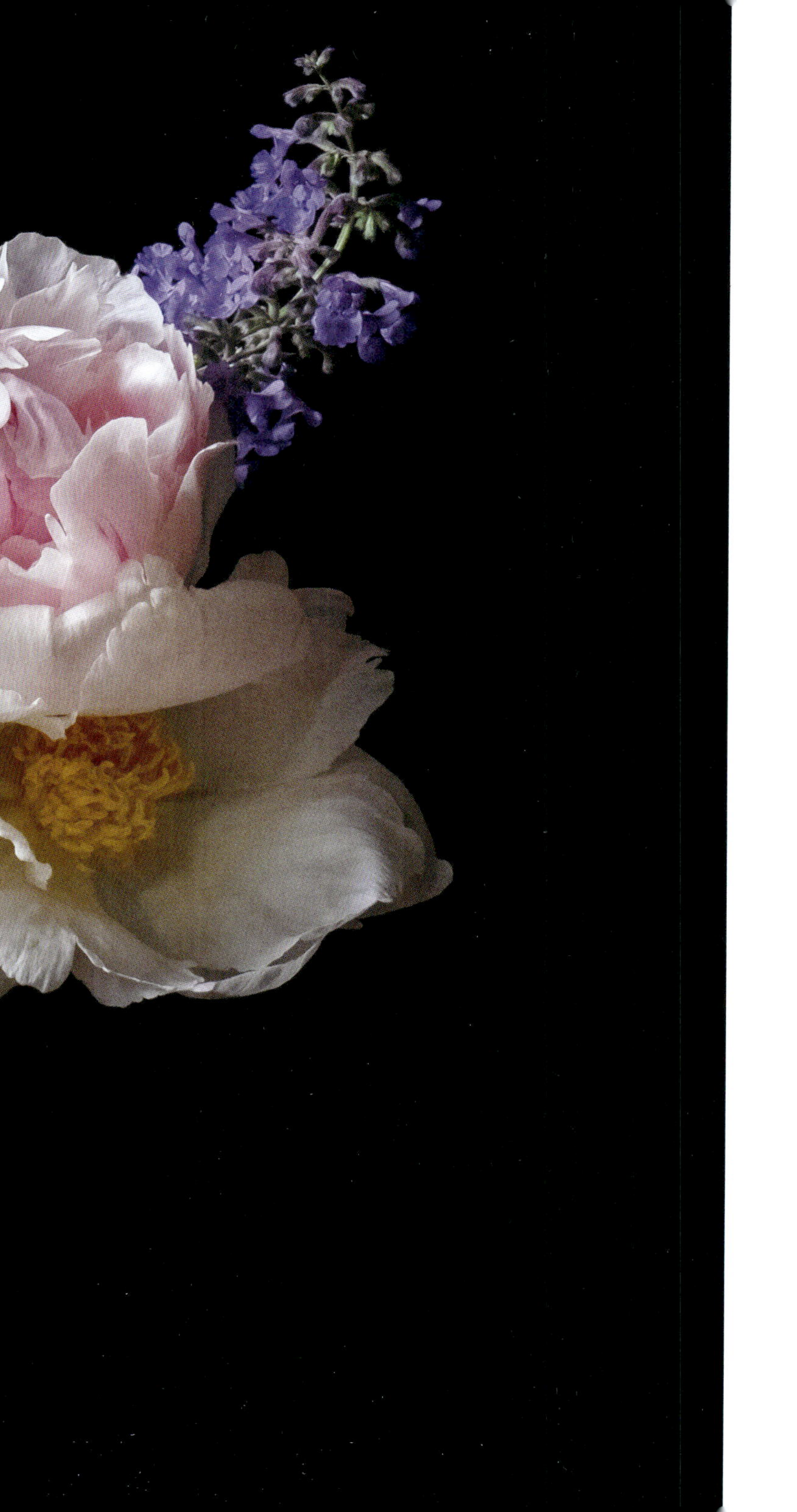

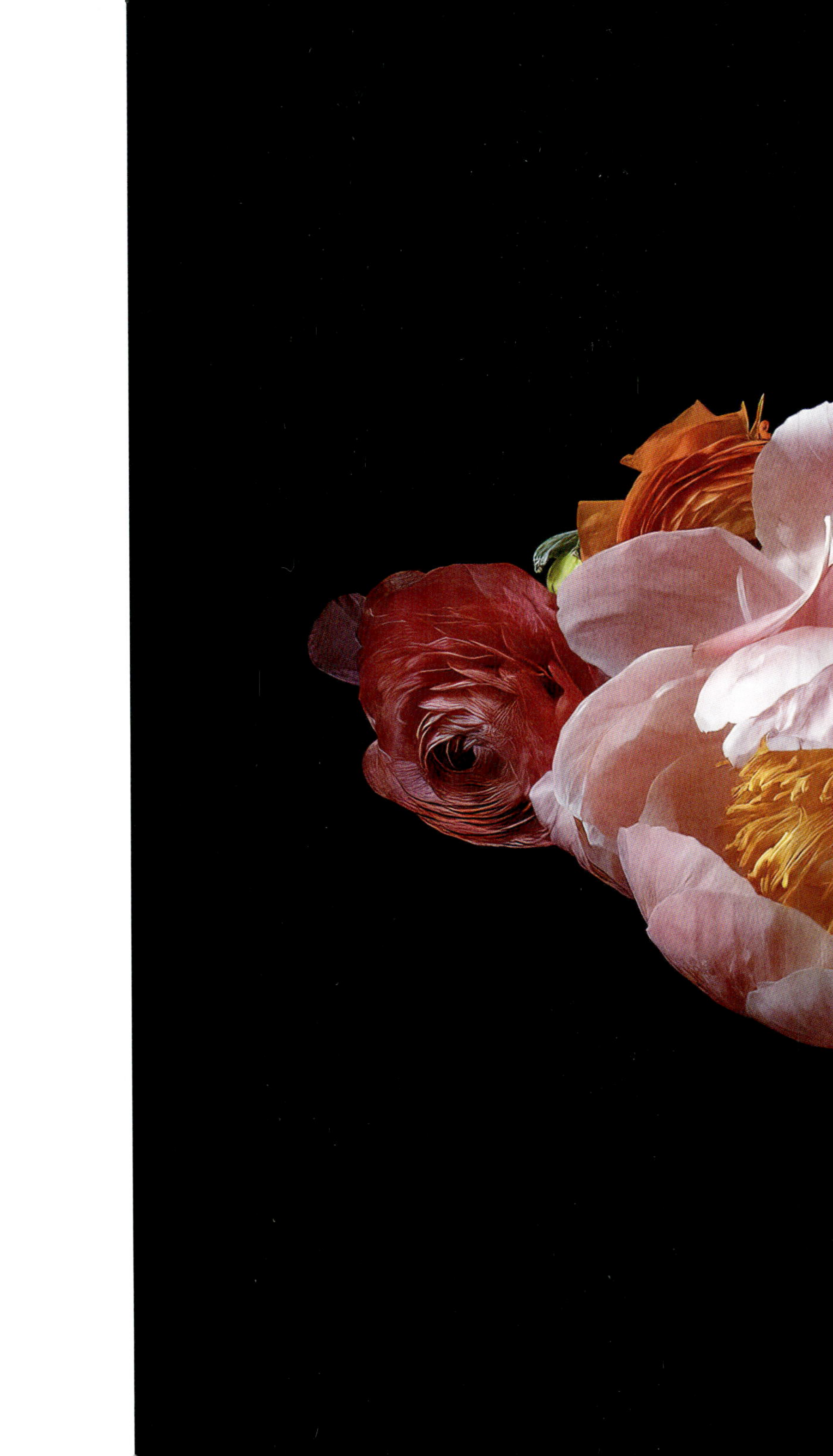

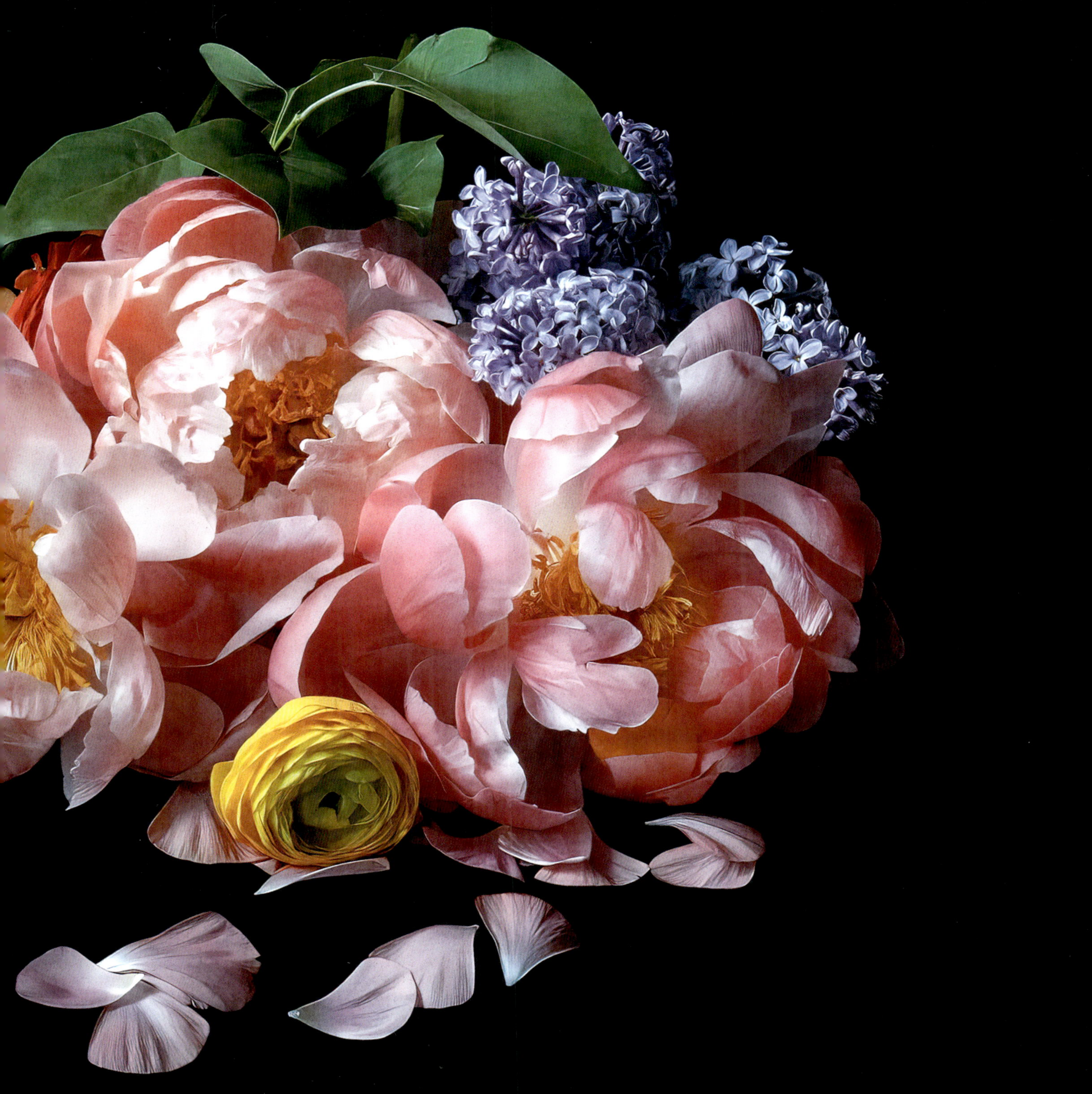

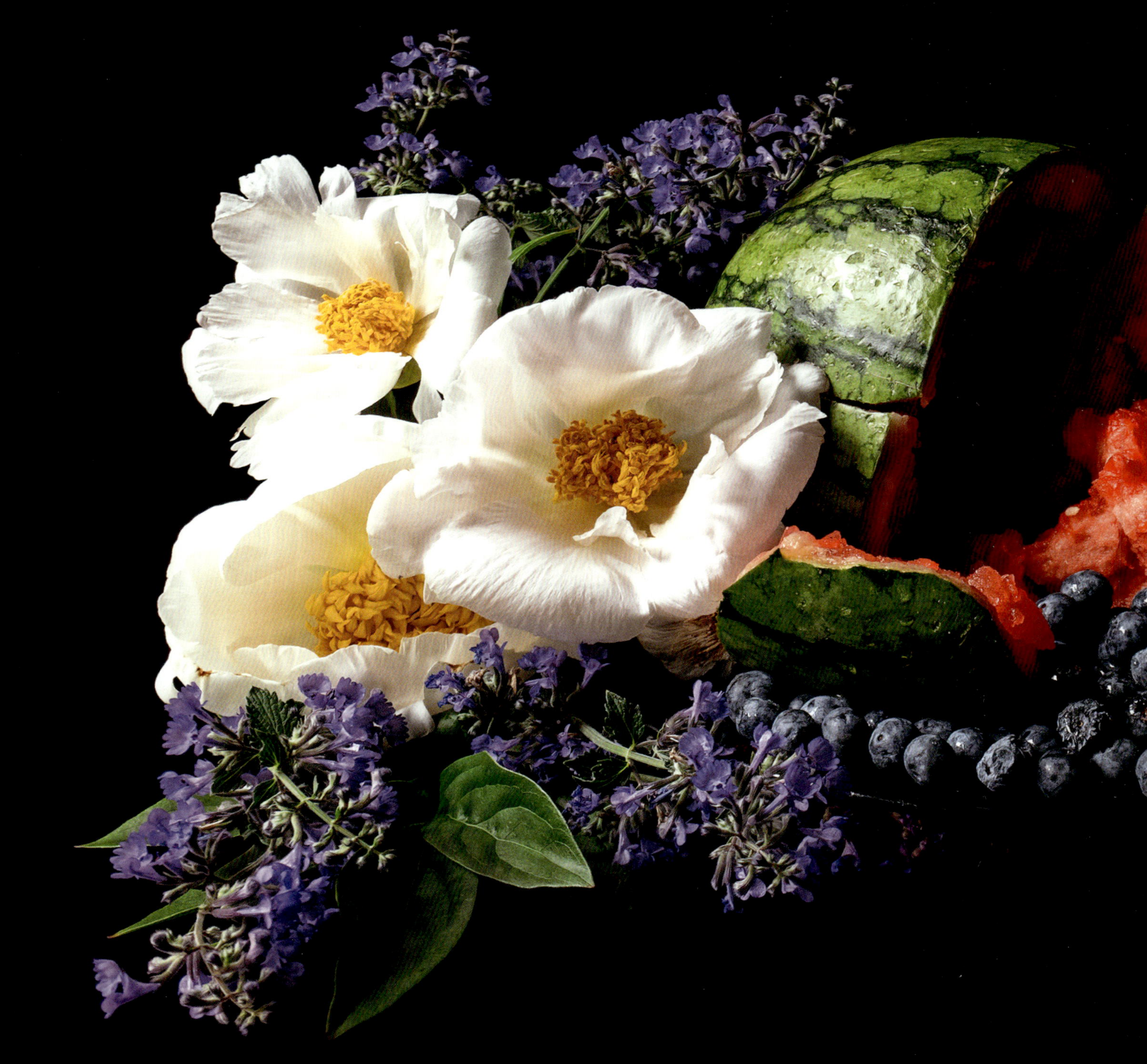

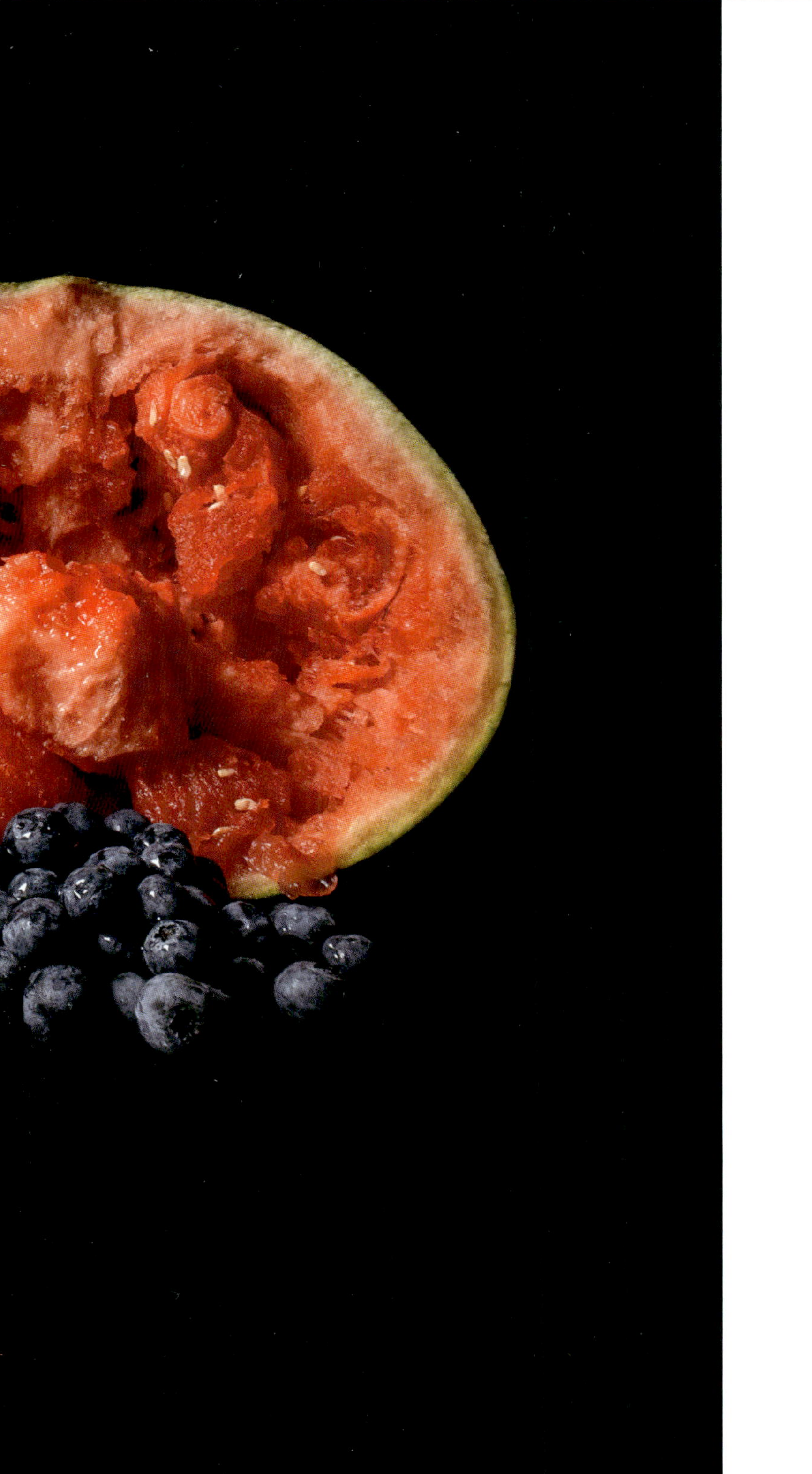

I meant to go out for a walk.
I got lost, then found, in the garden.

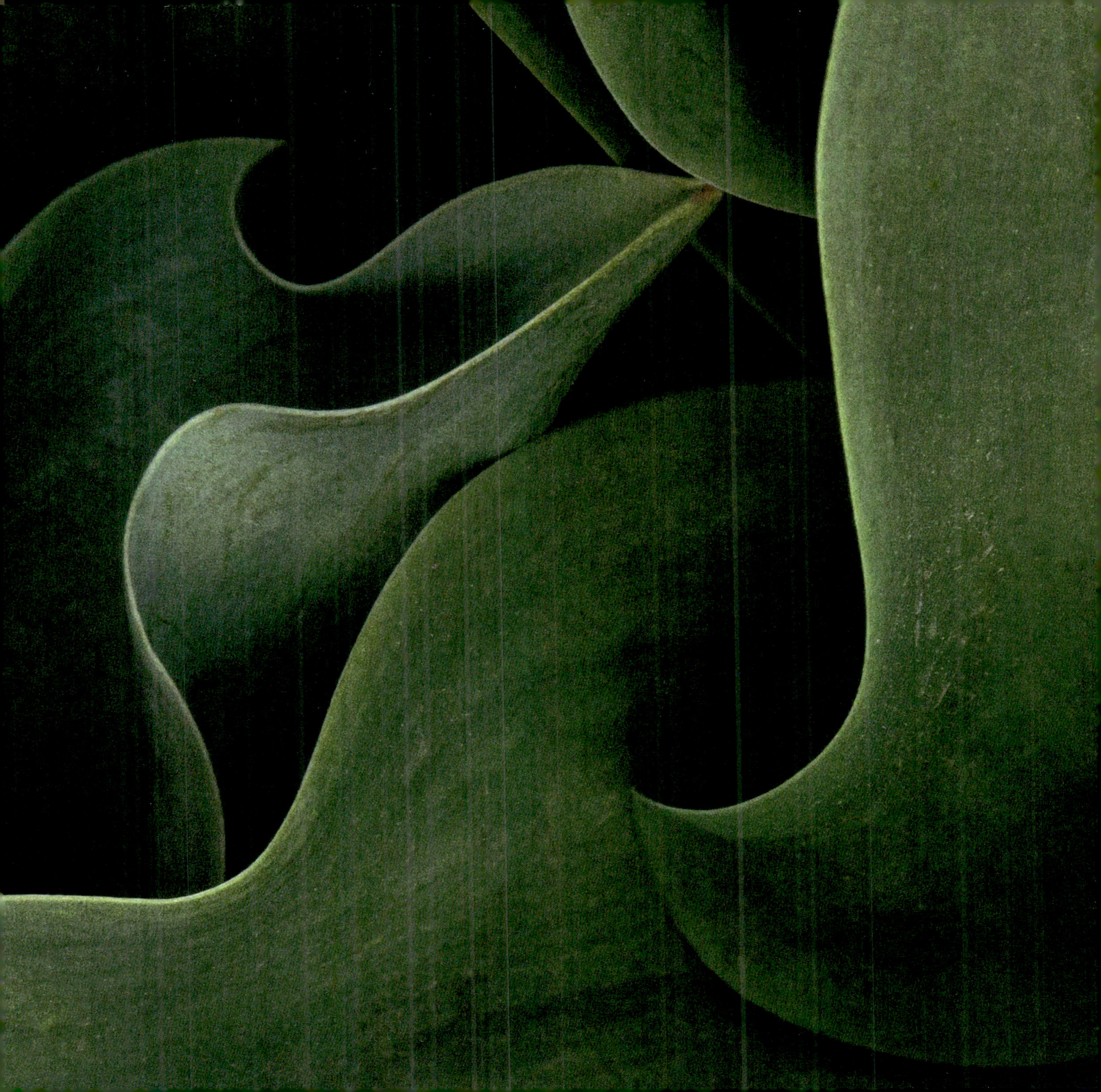

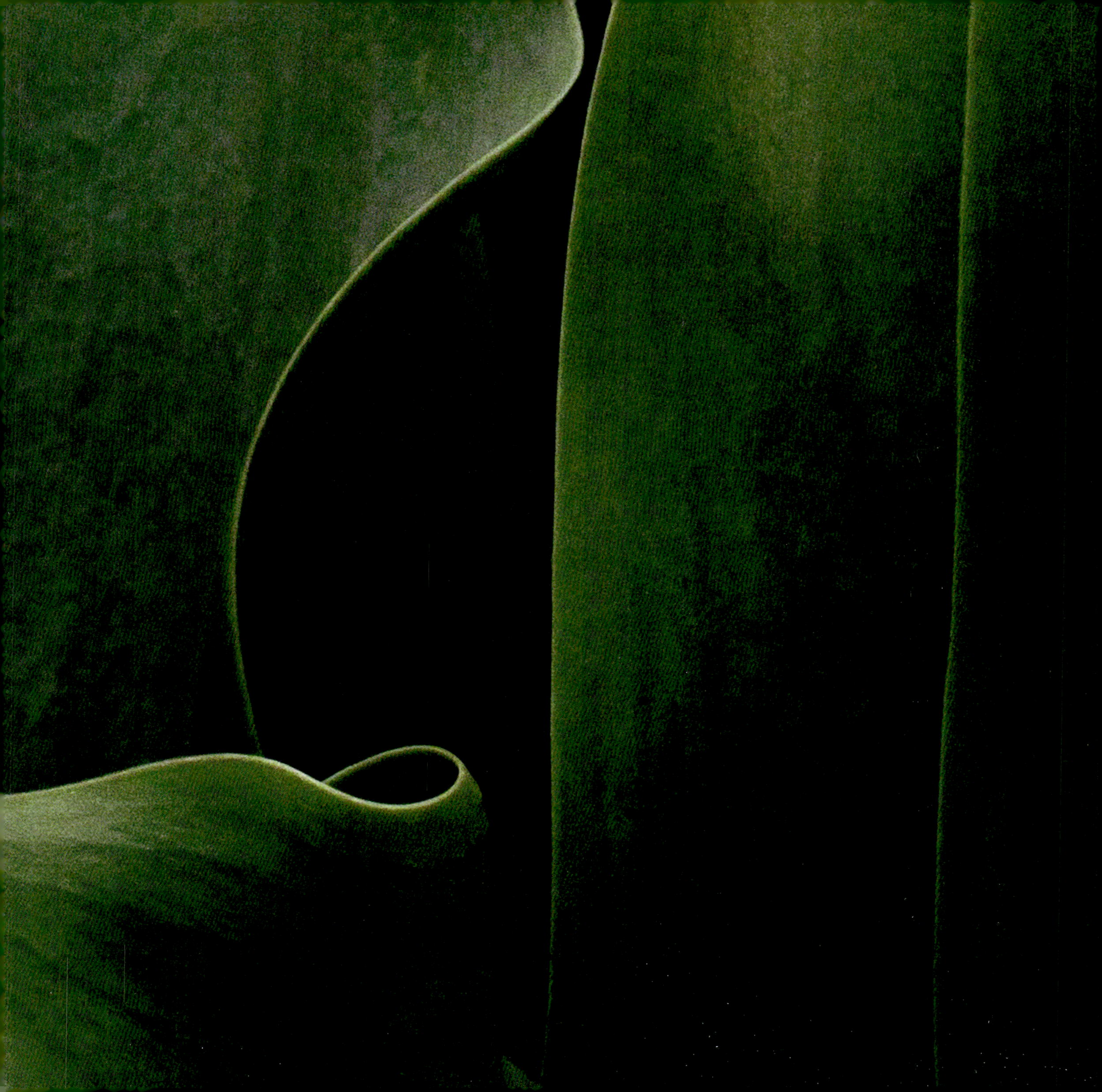

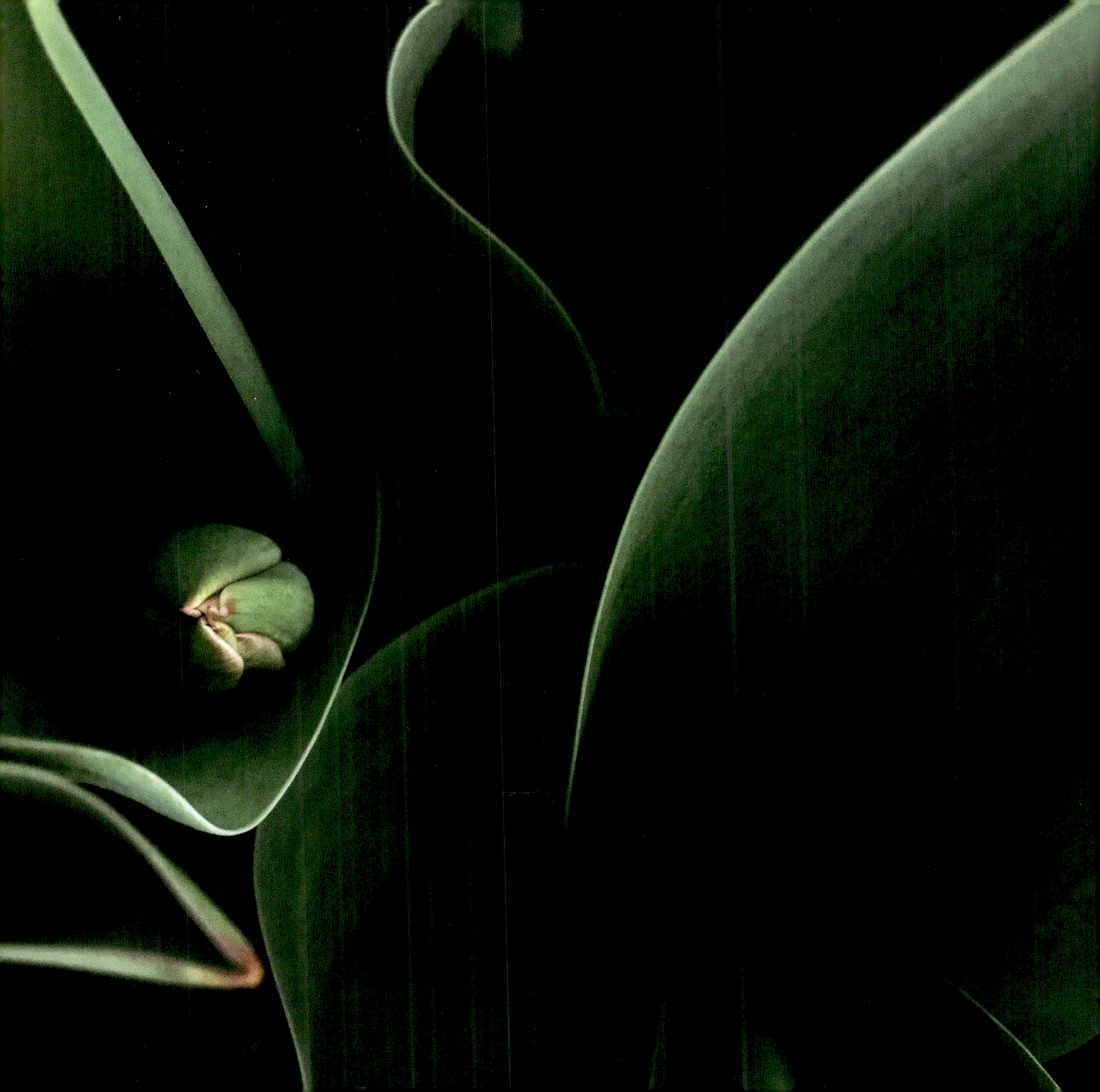

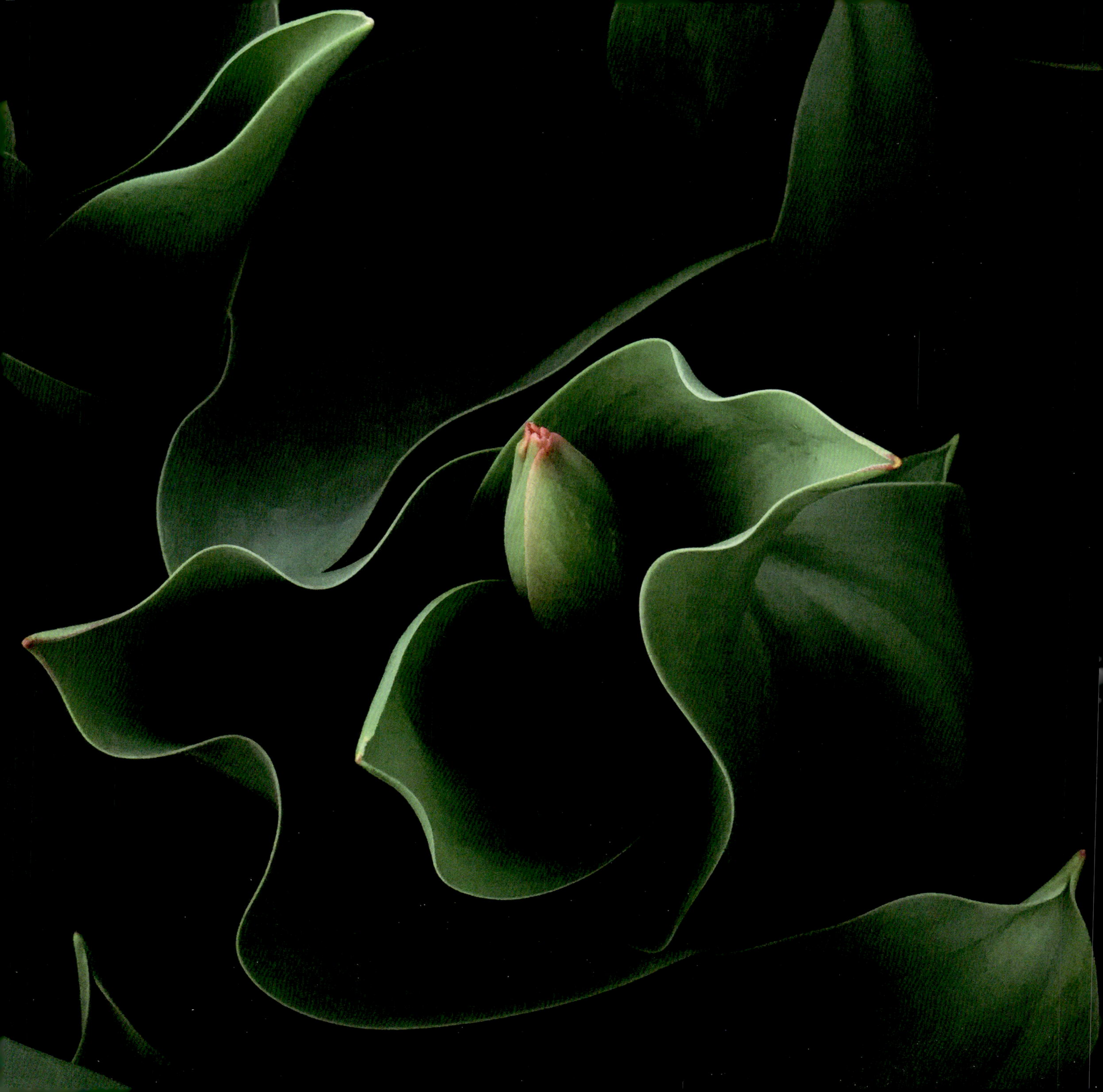

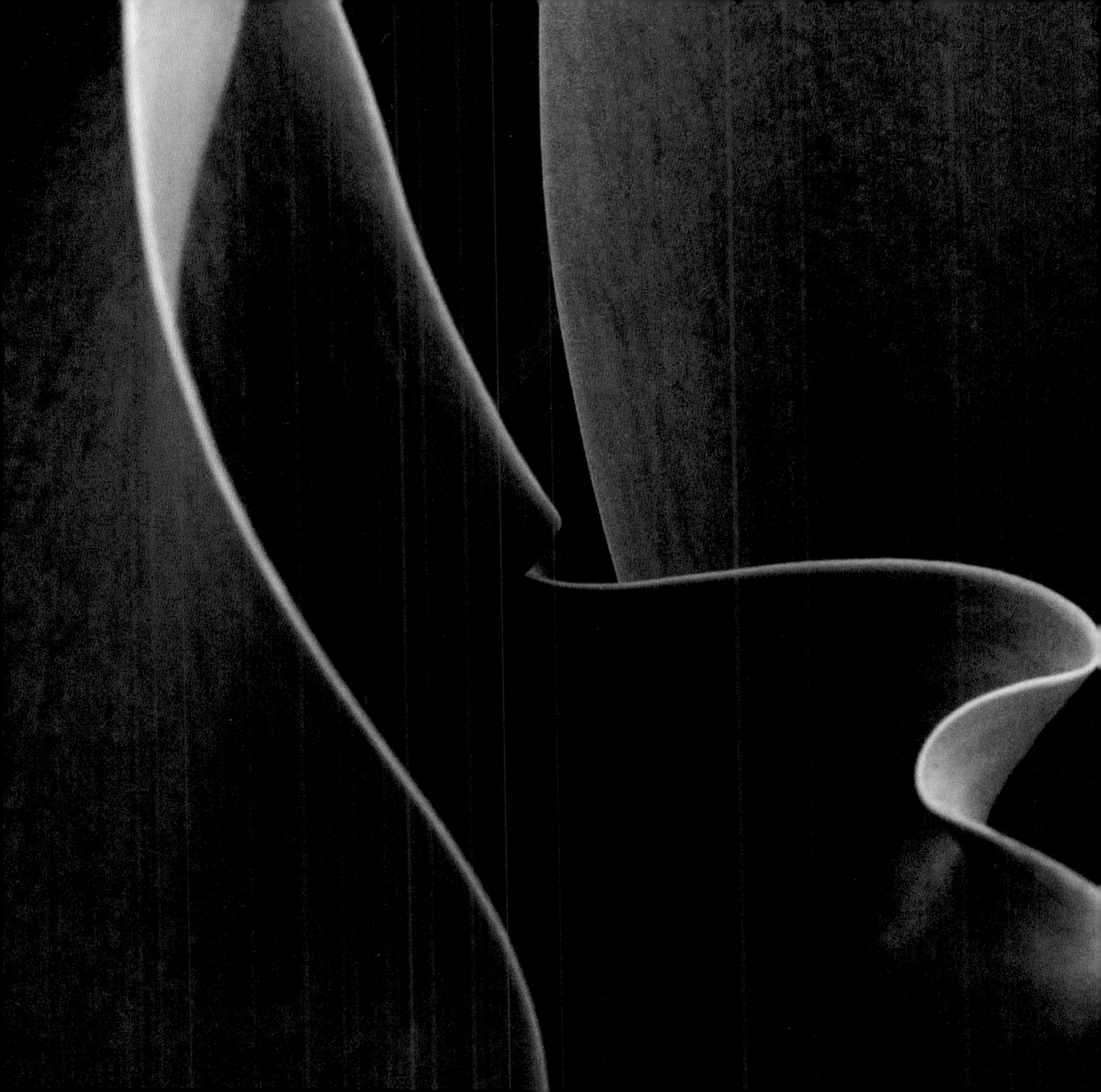

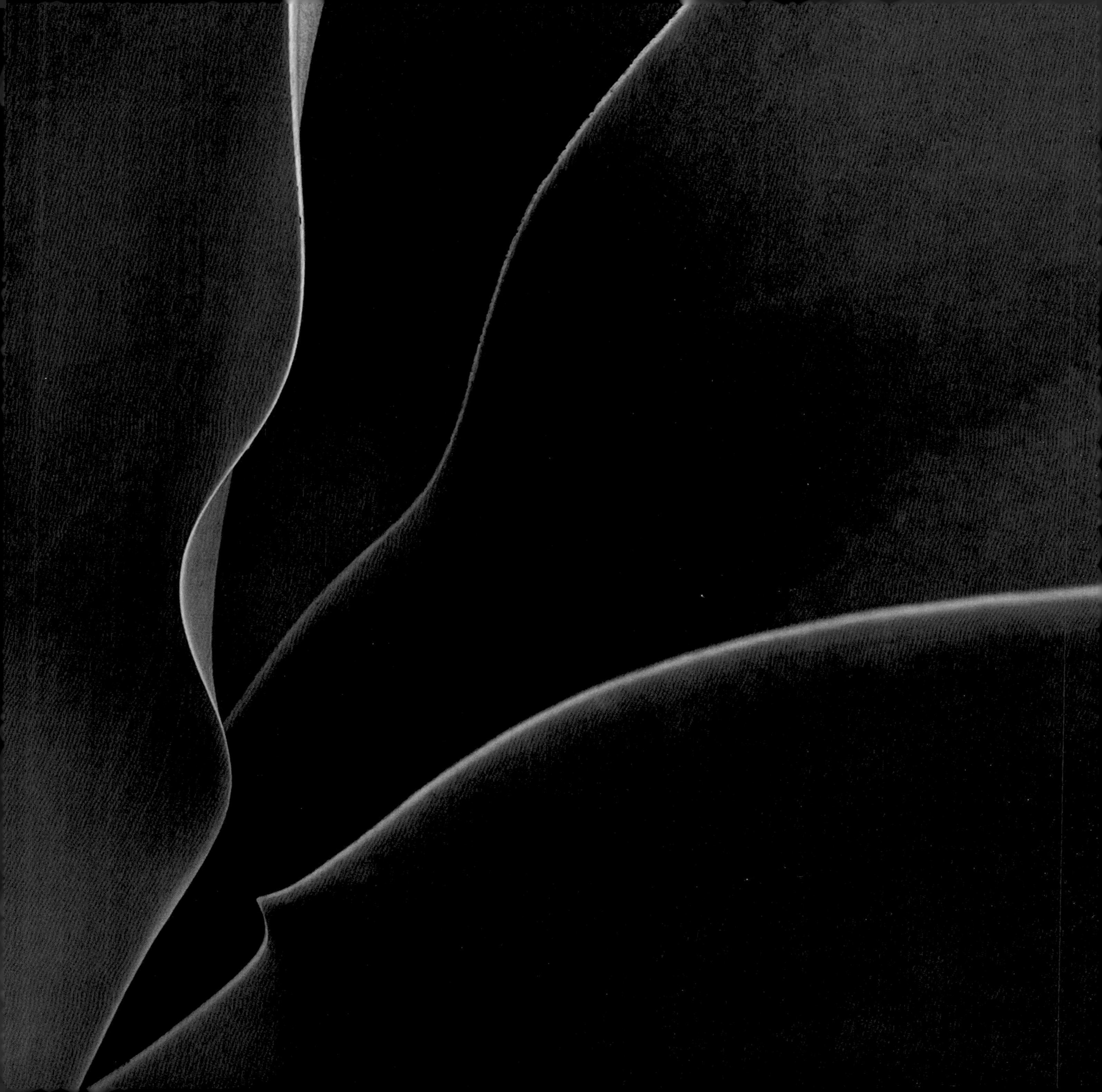

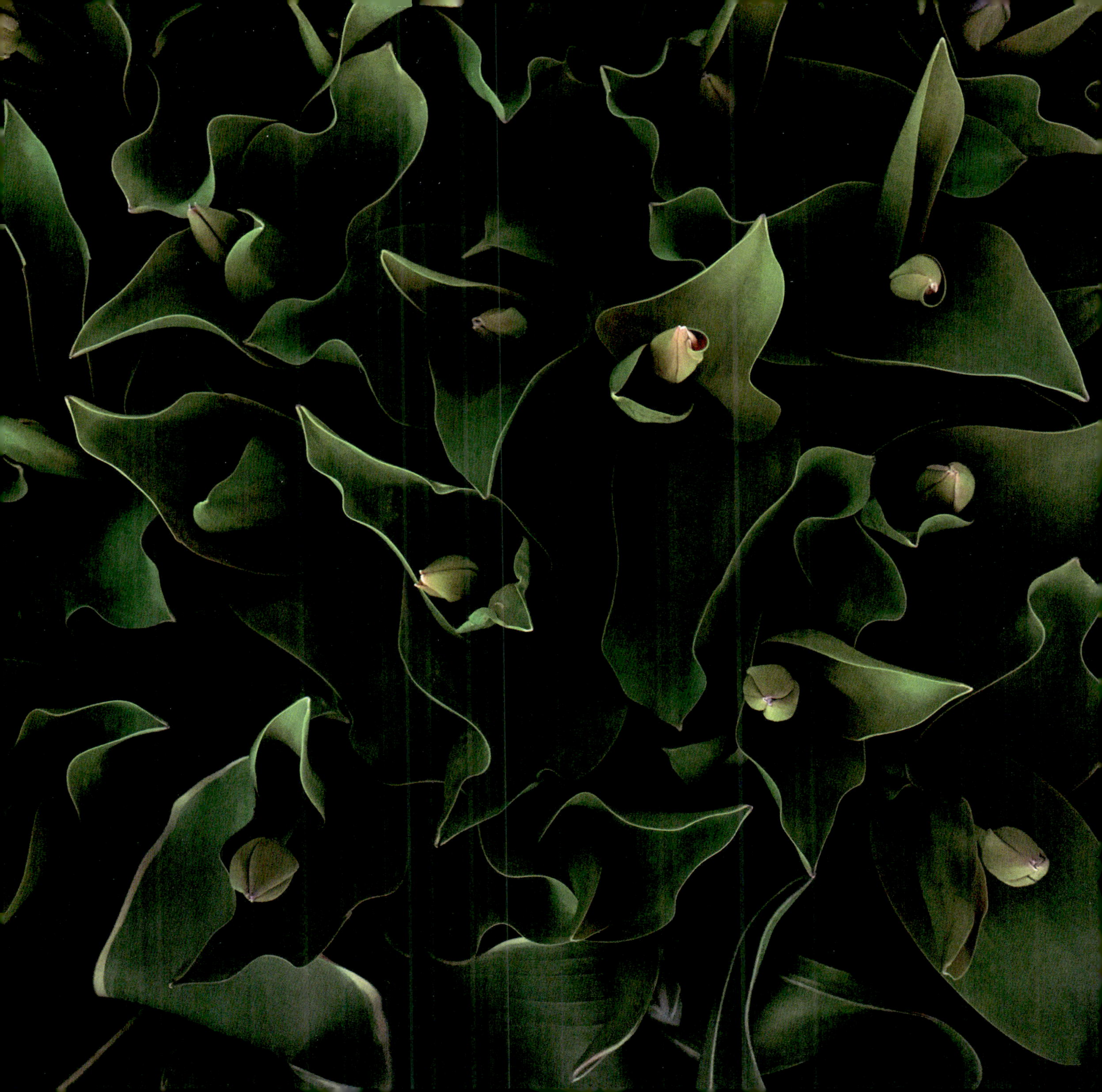

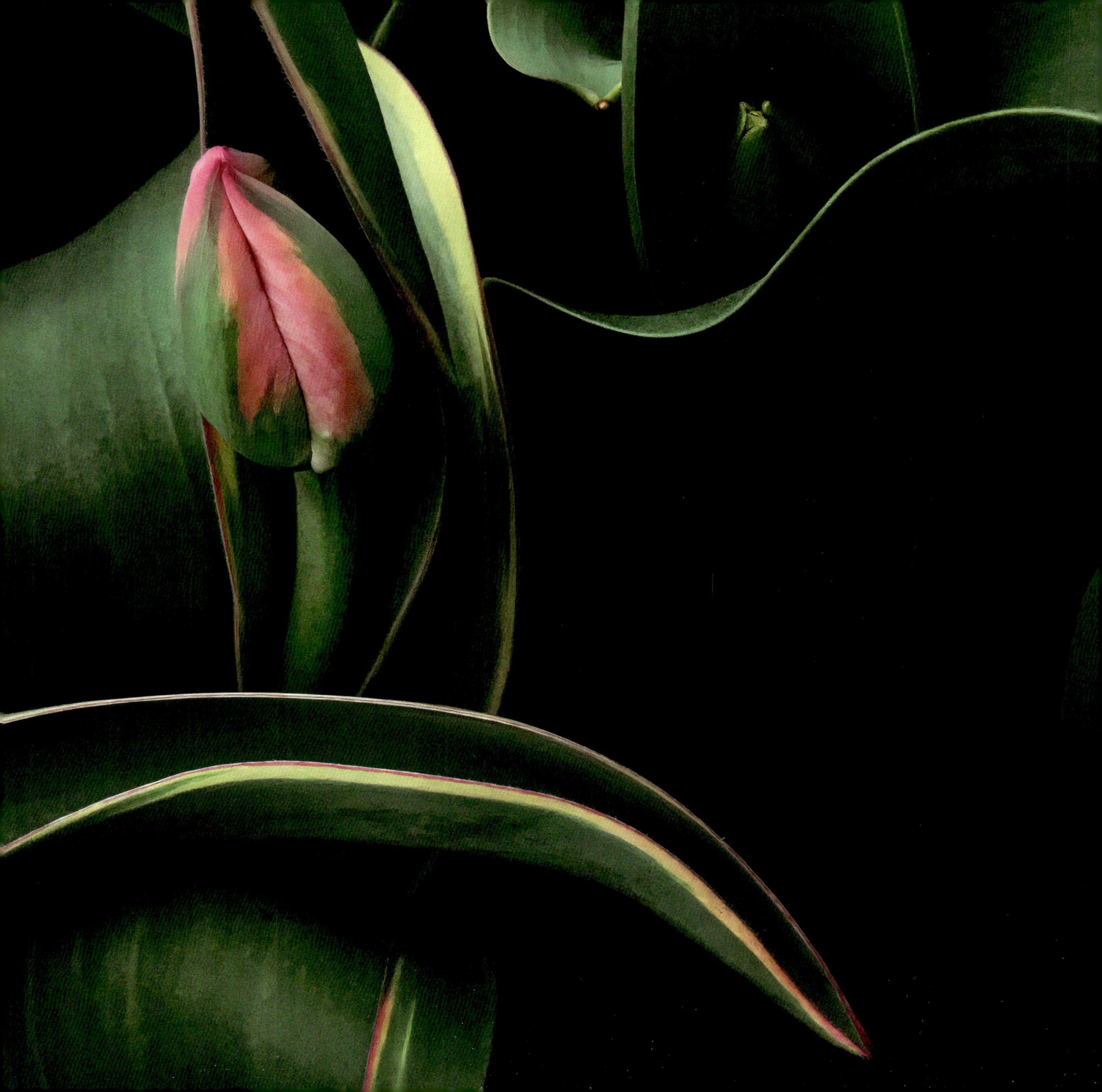

The gardens are a refuge I never anticipated.

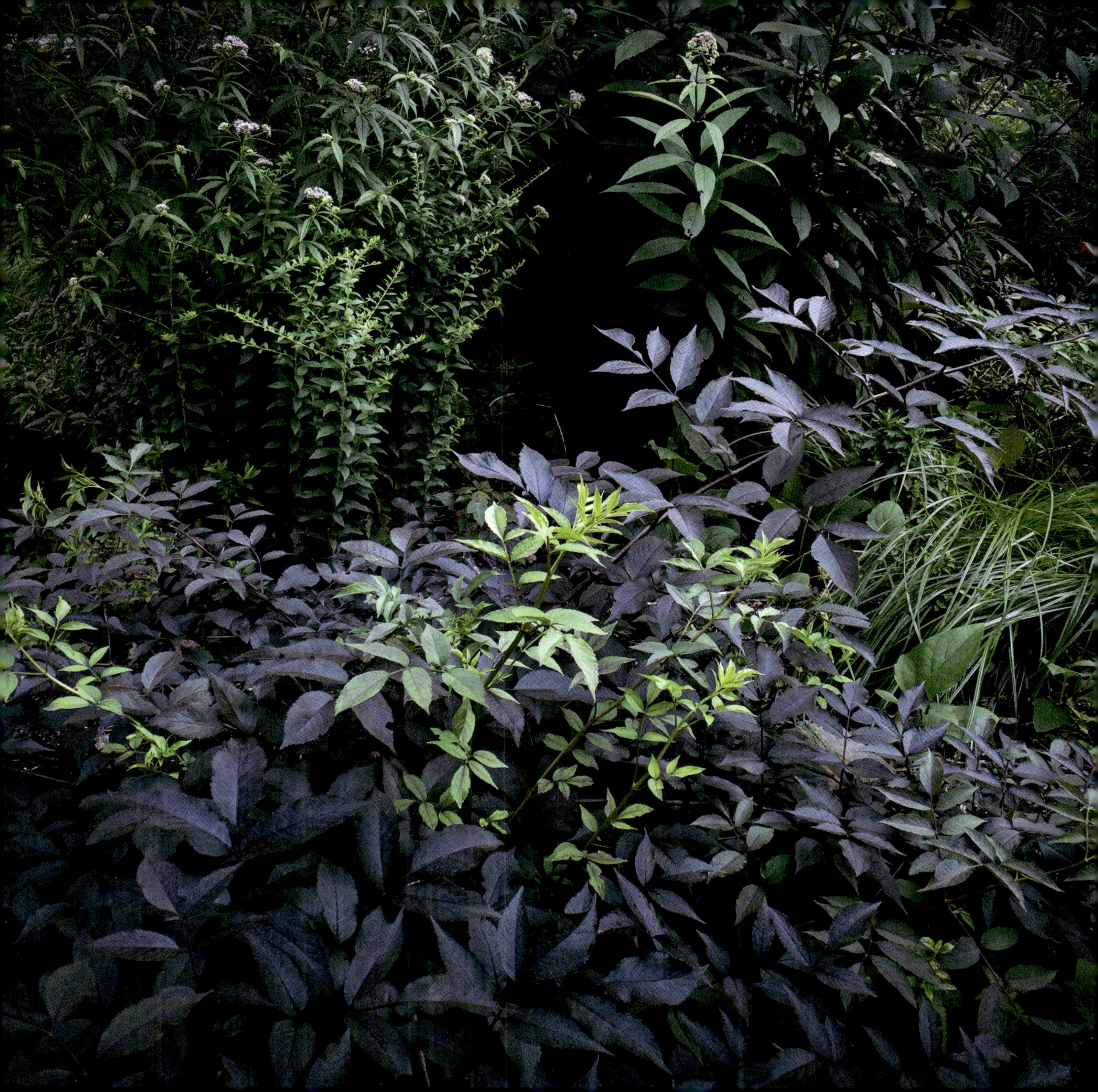

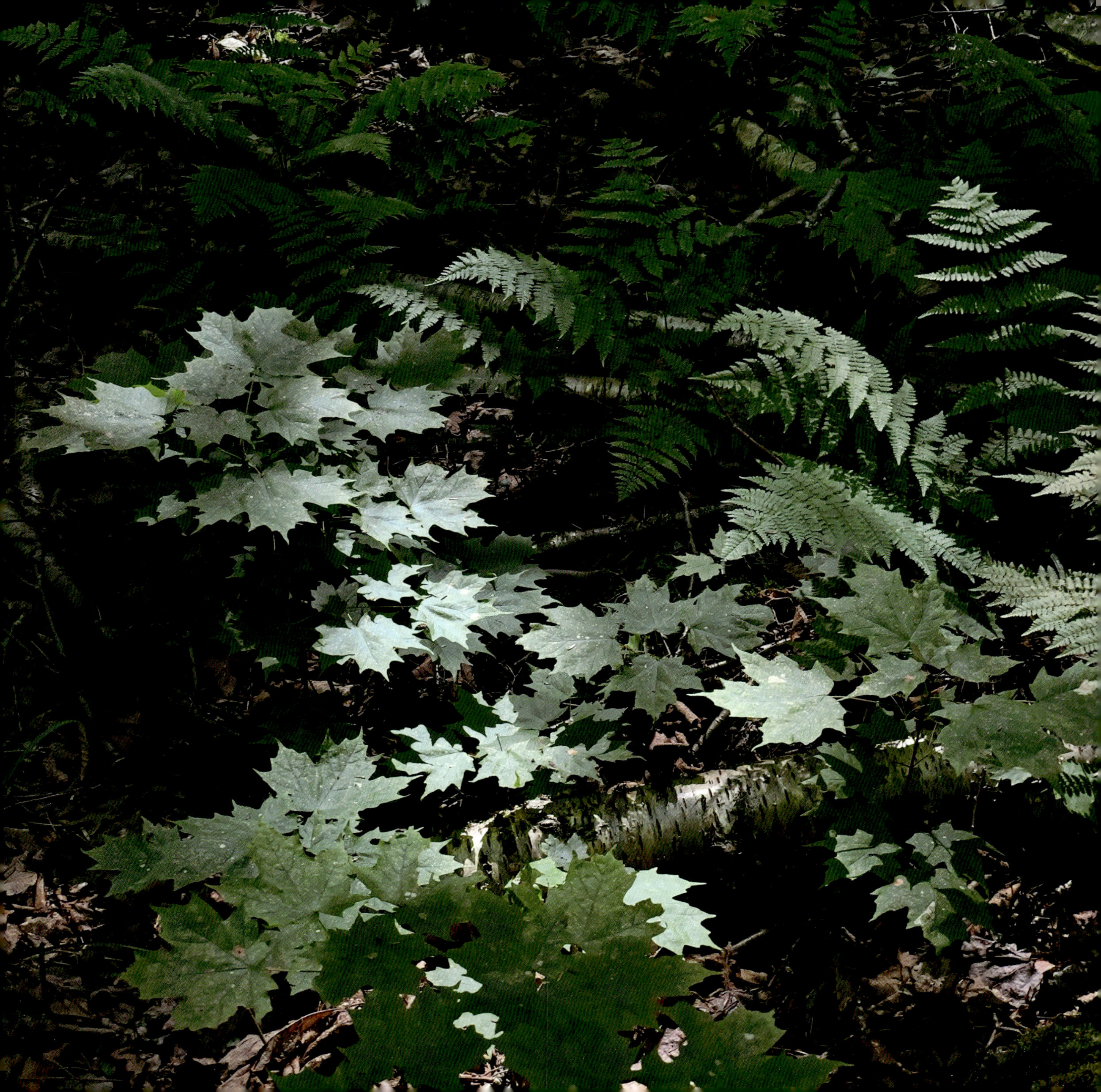

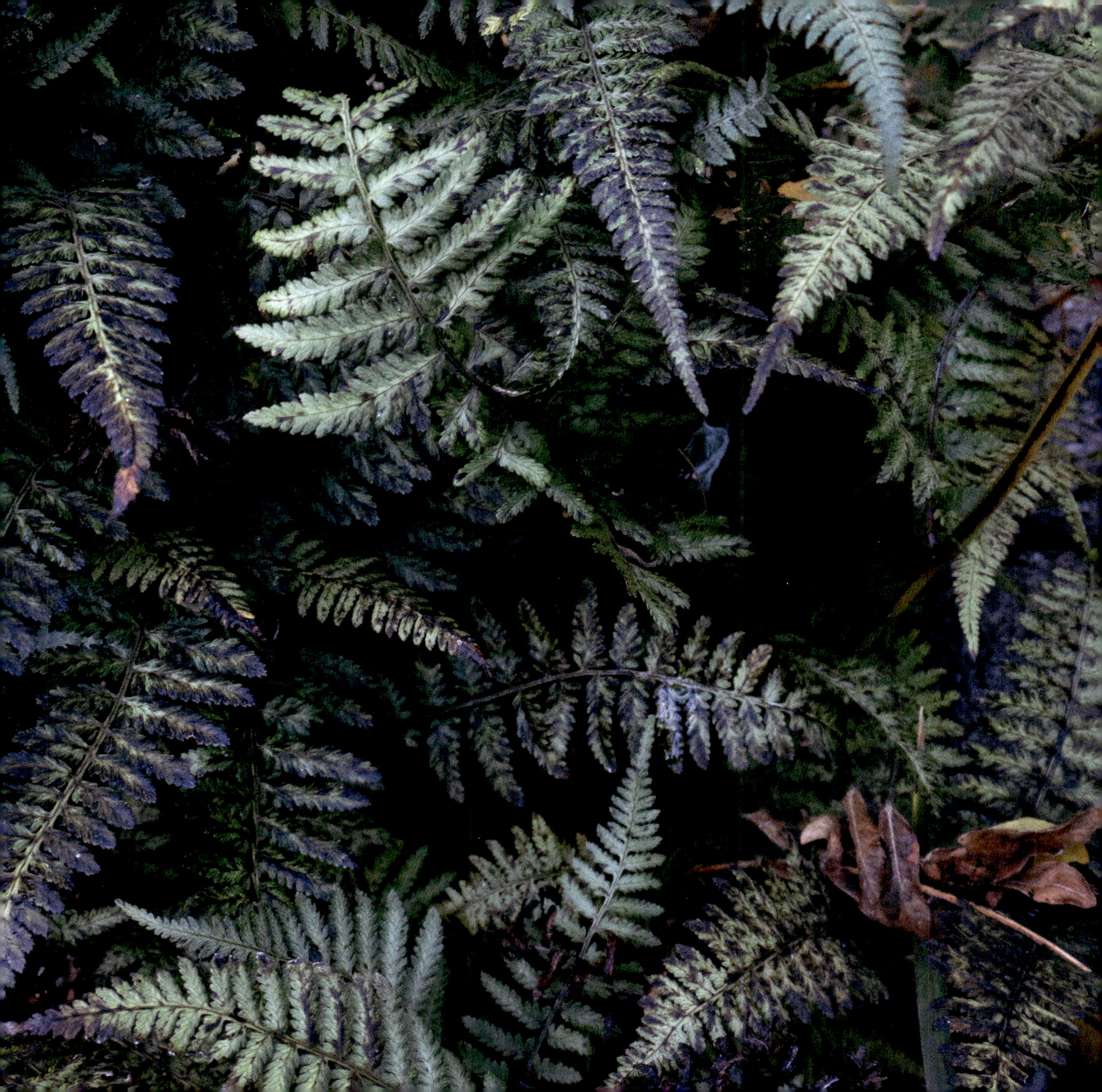

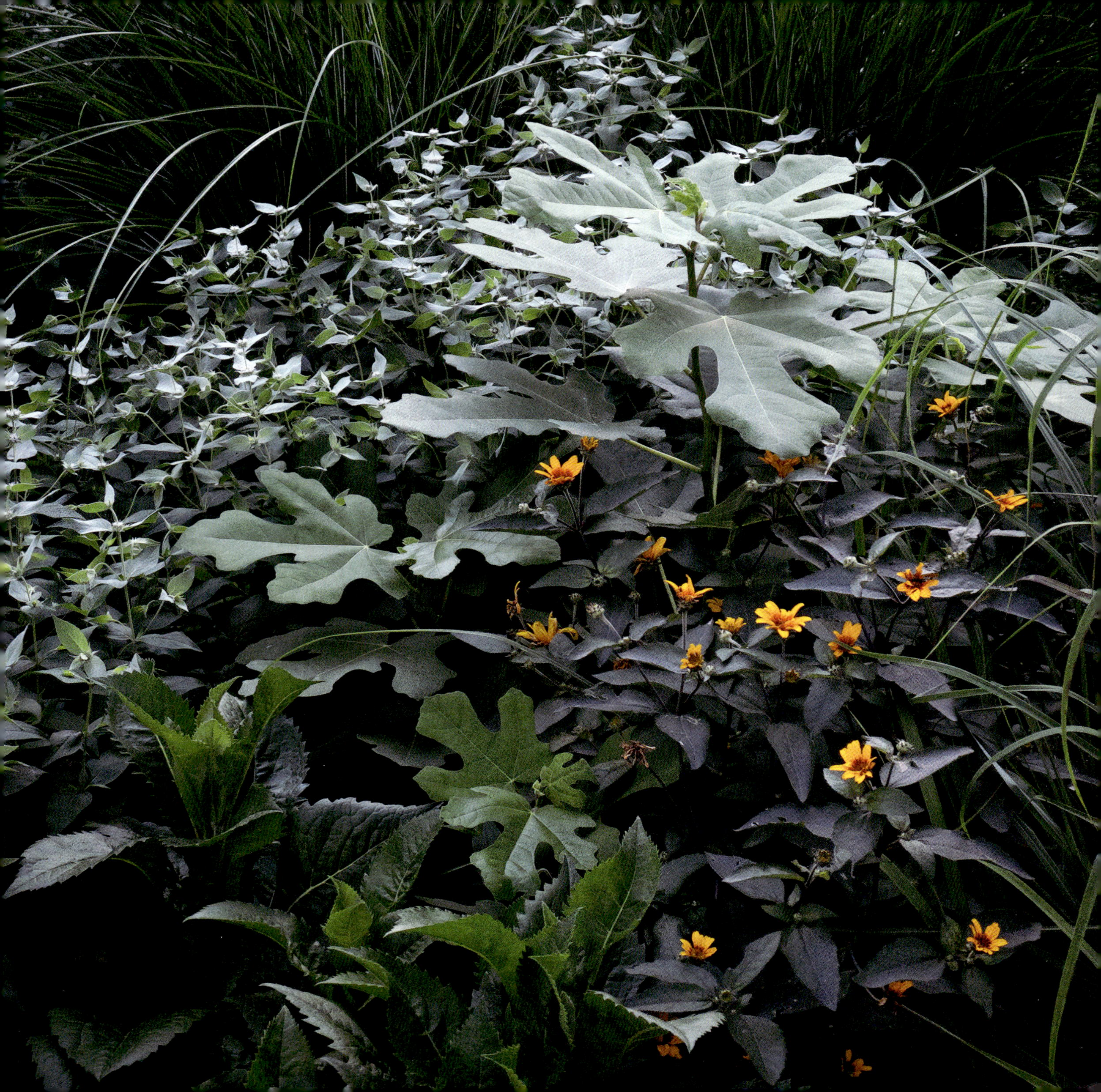

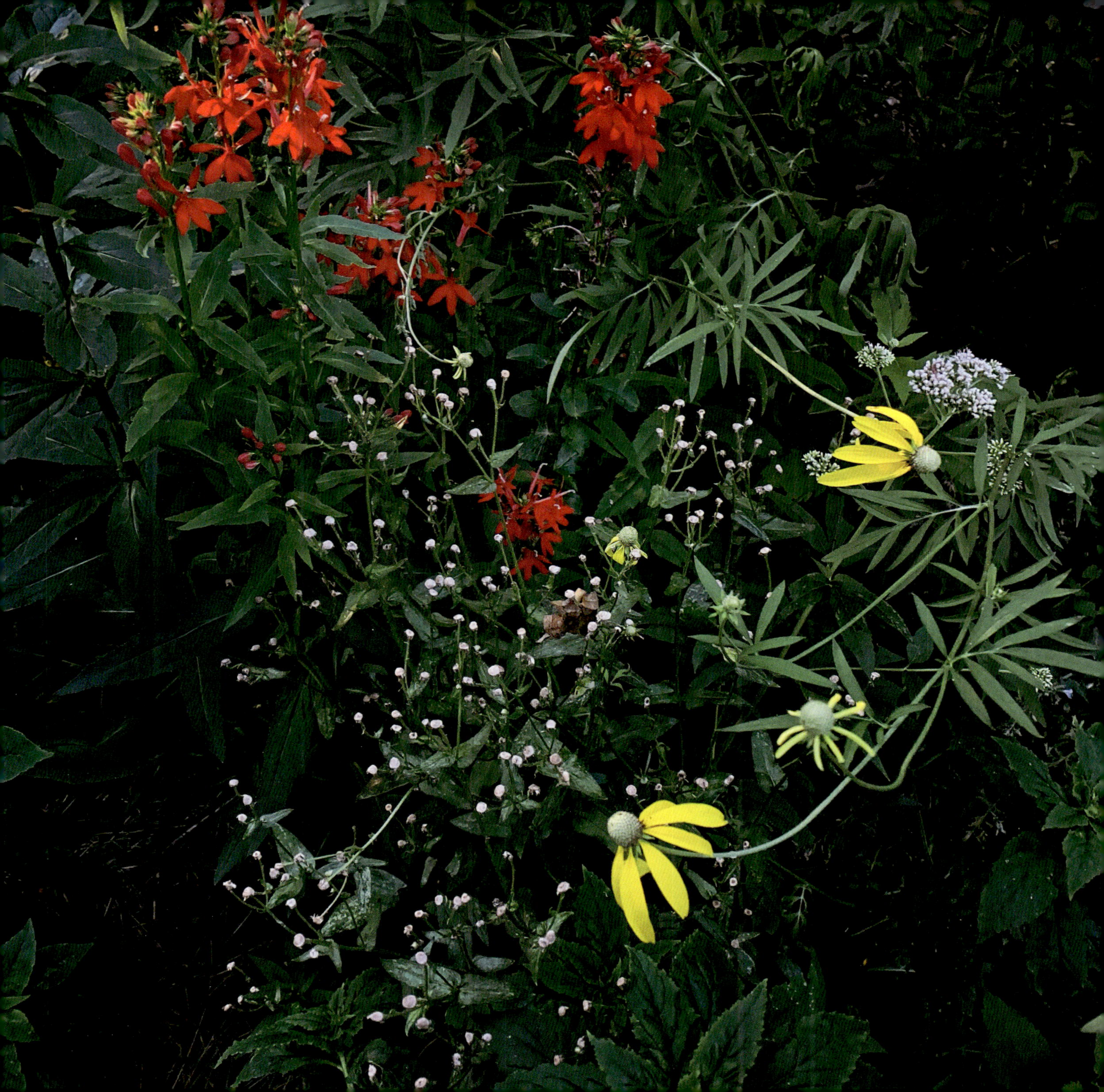

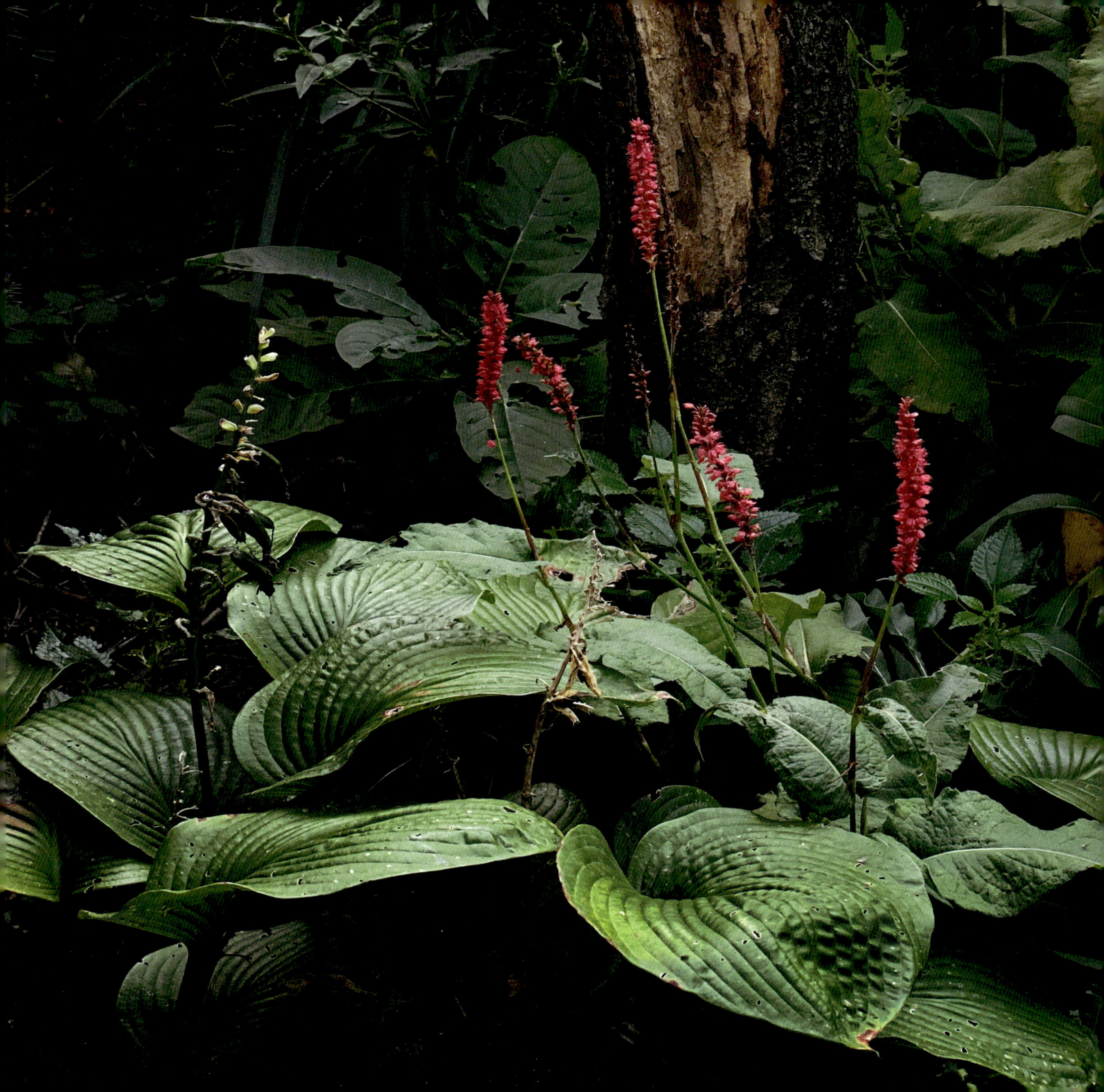

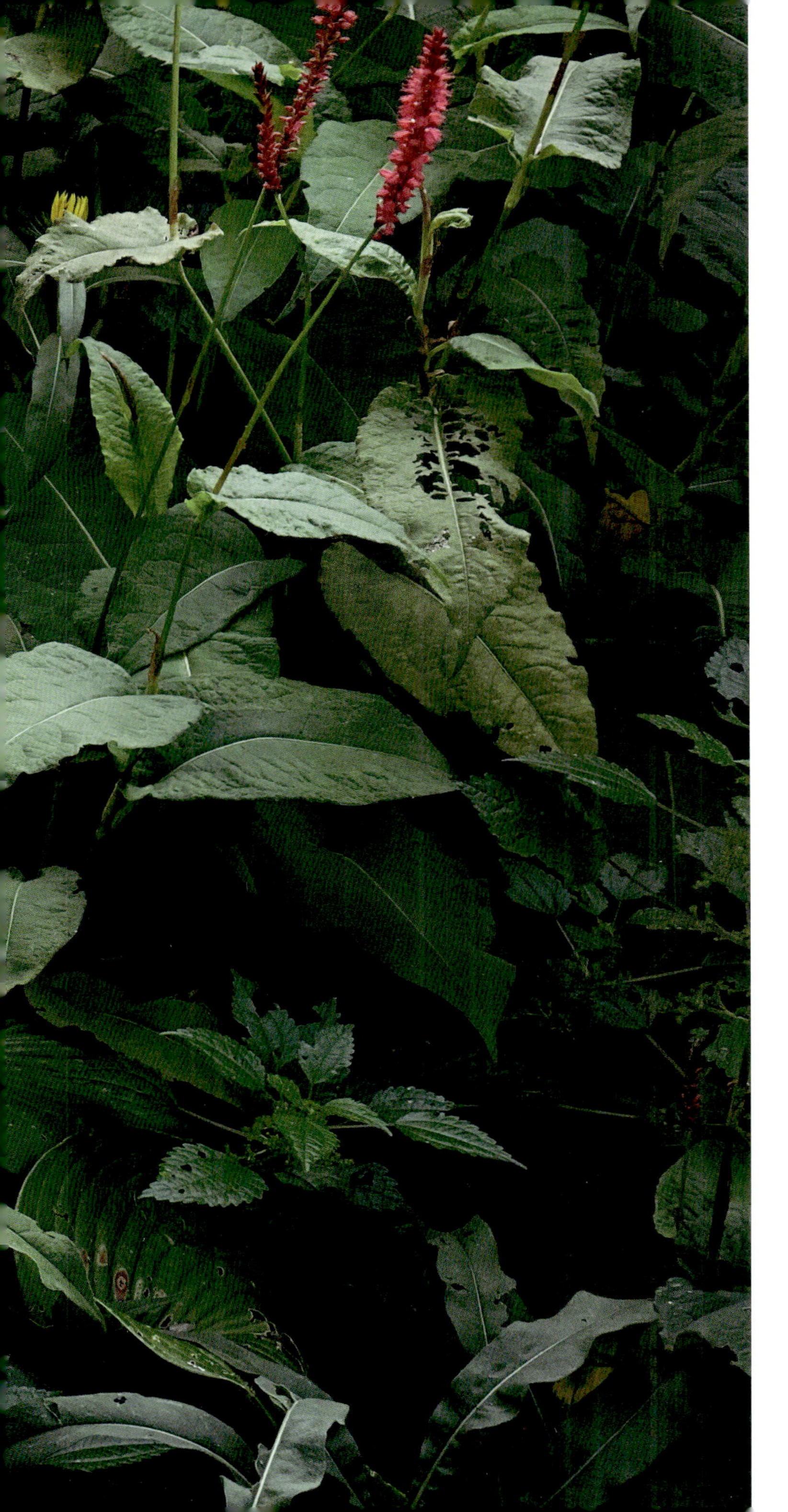

When I slow down, the world offers itself
up in ways I never could have imagined.
The past and the future cease to exist.
It is in the present moment that I can see anew.

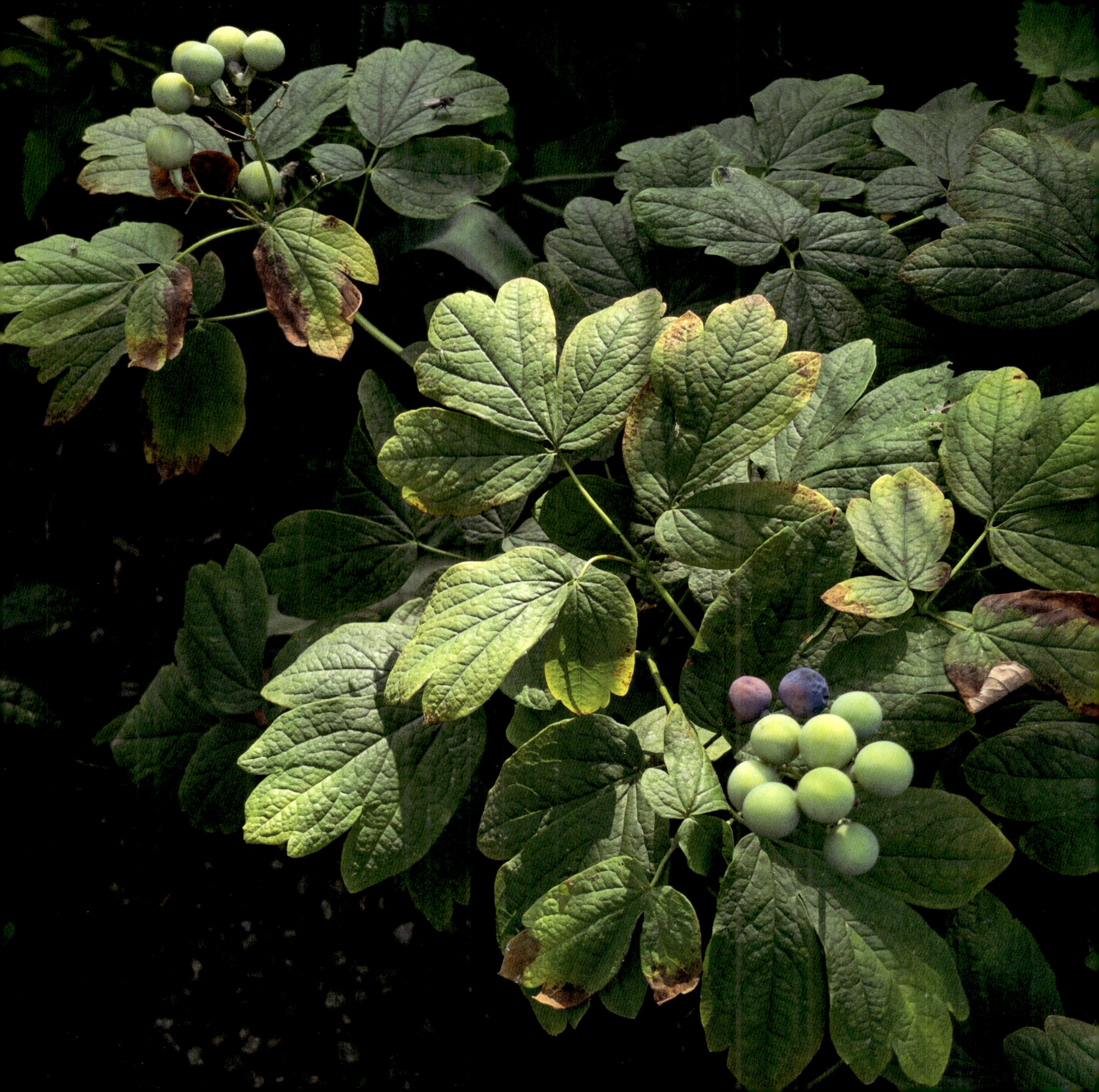

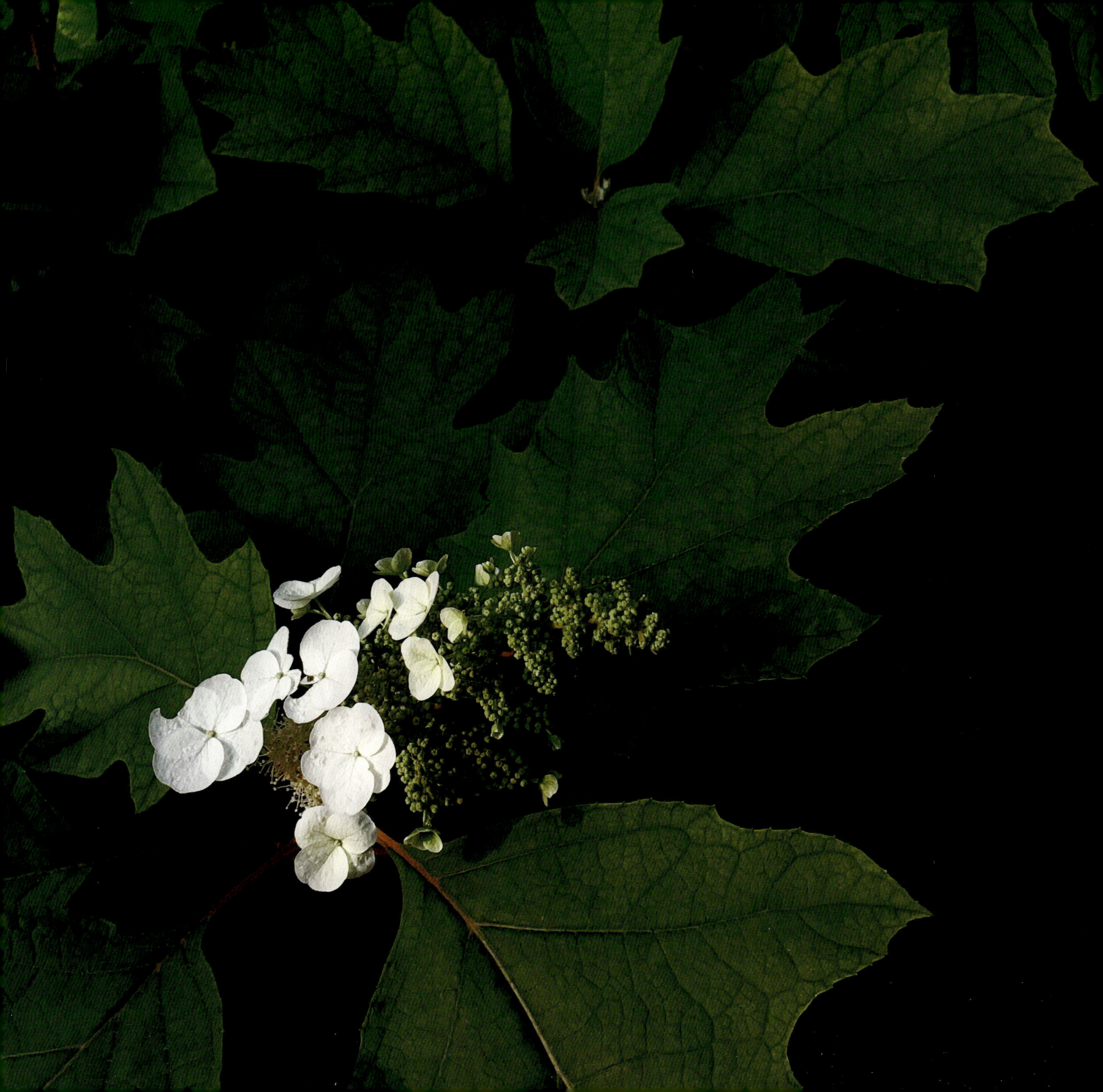

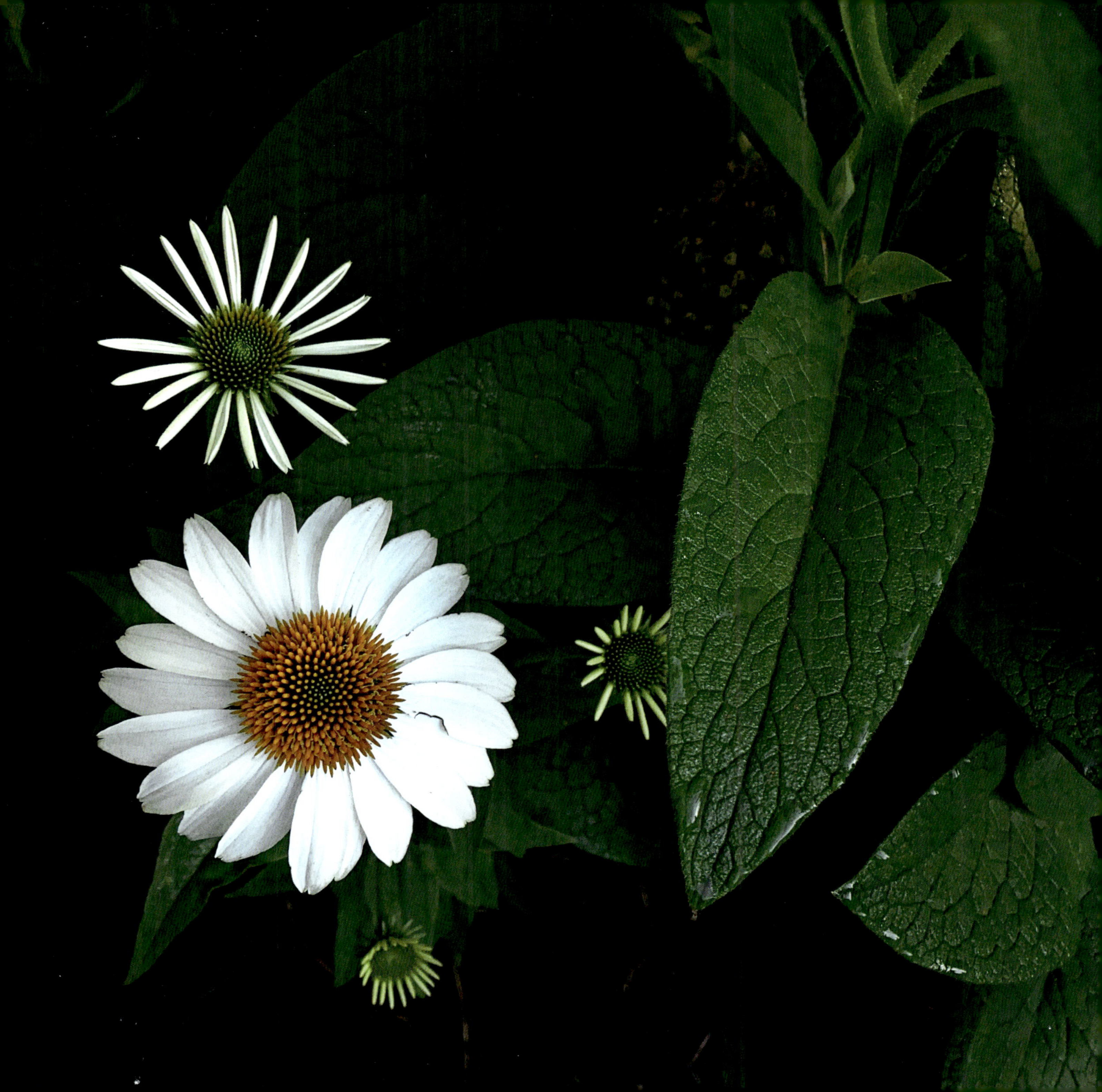

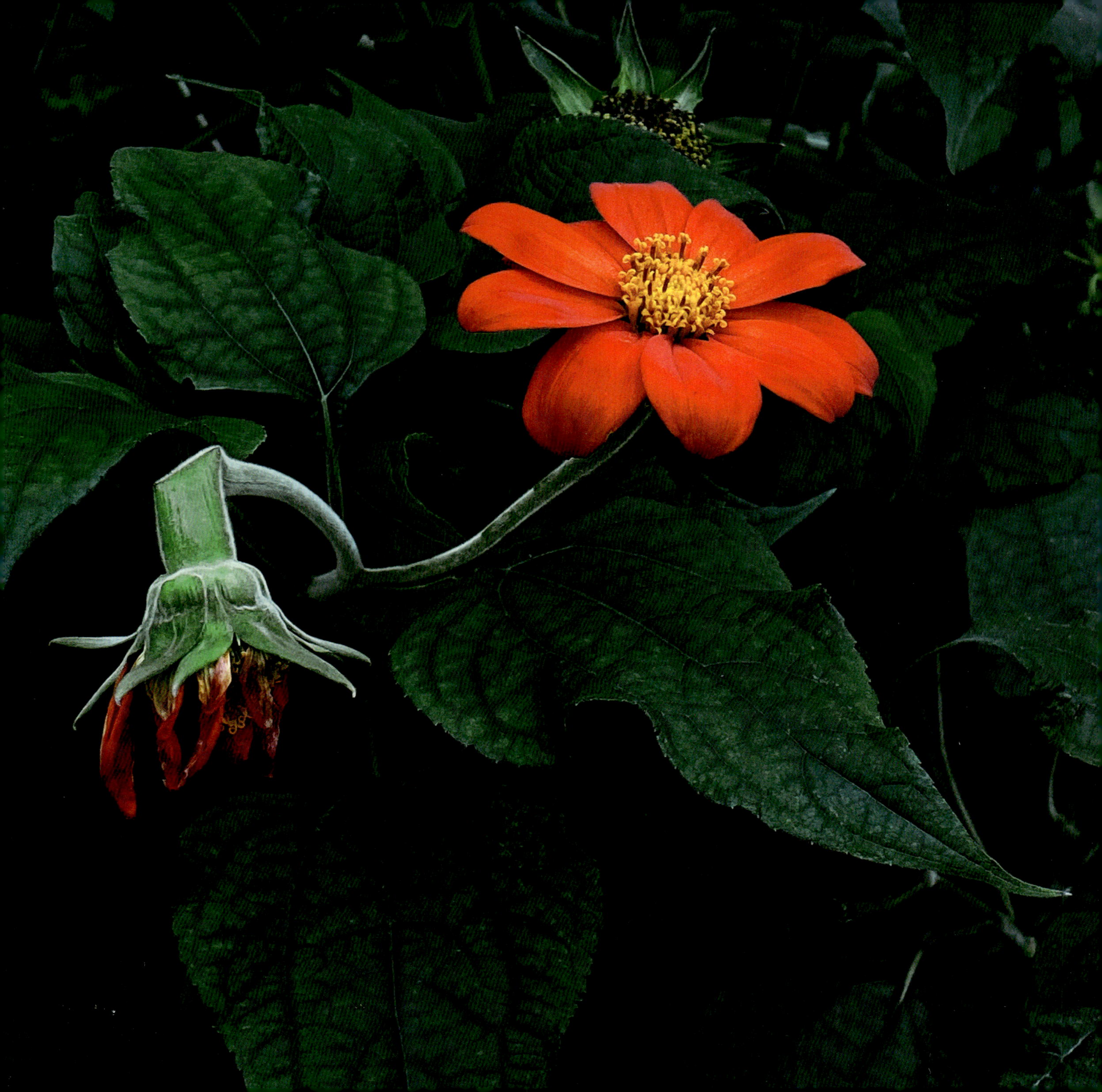

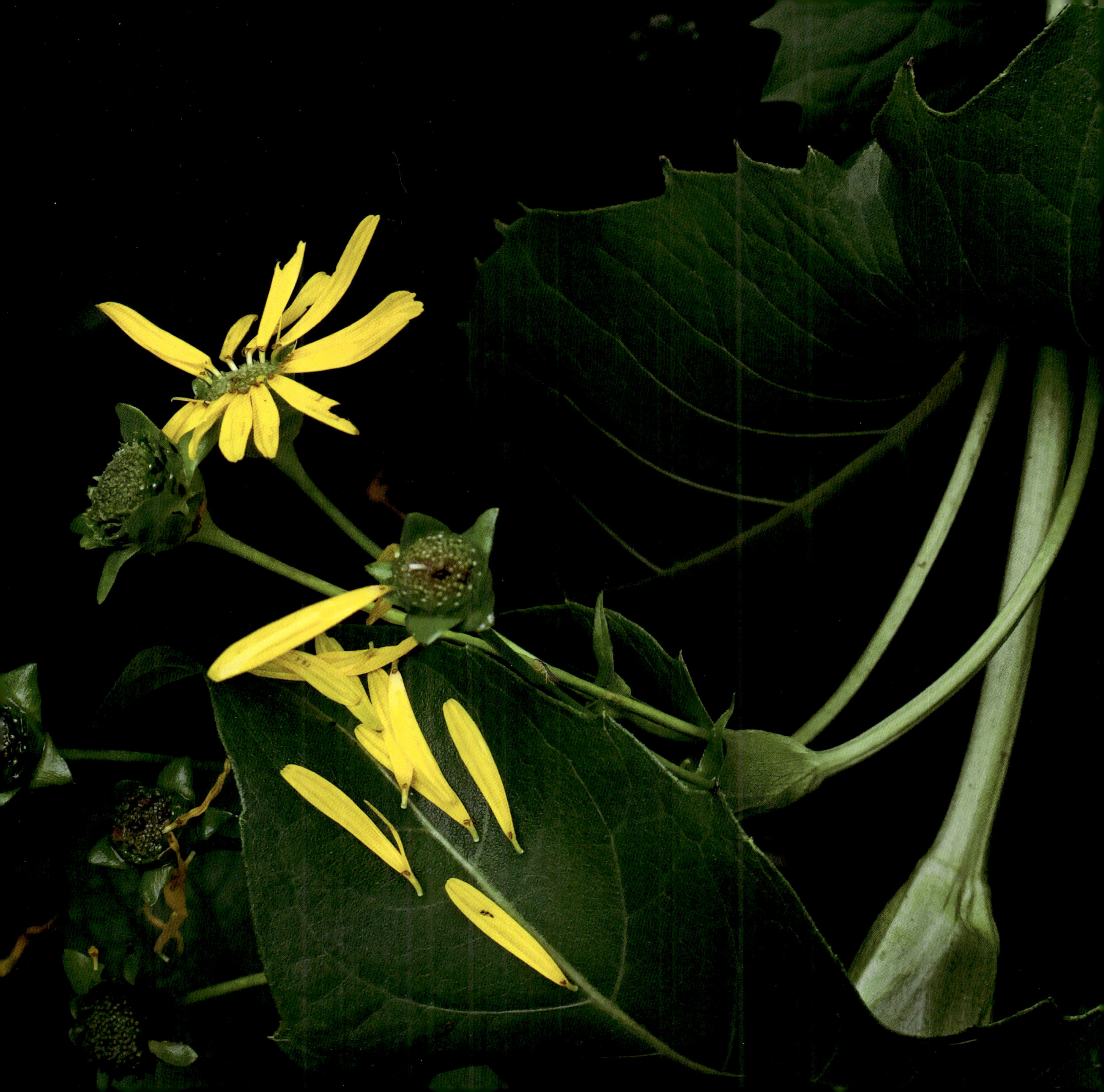

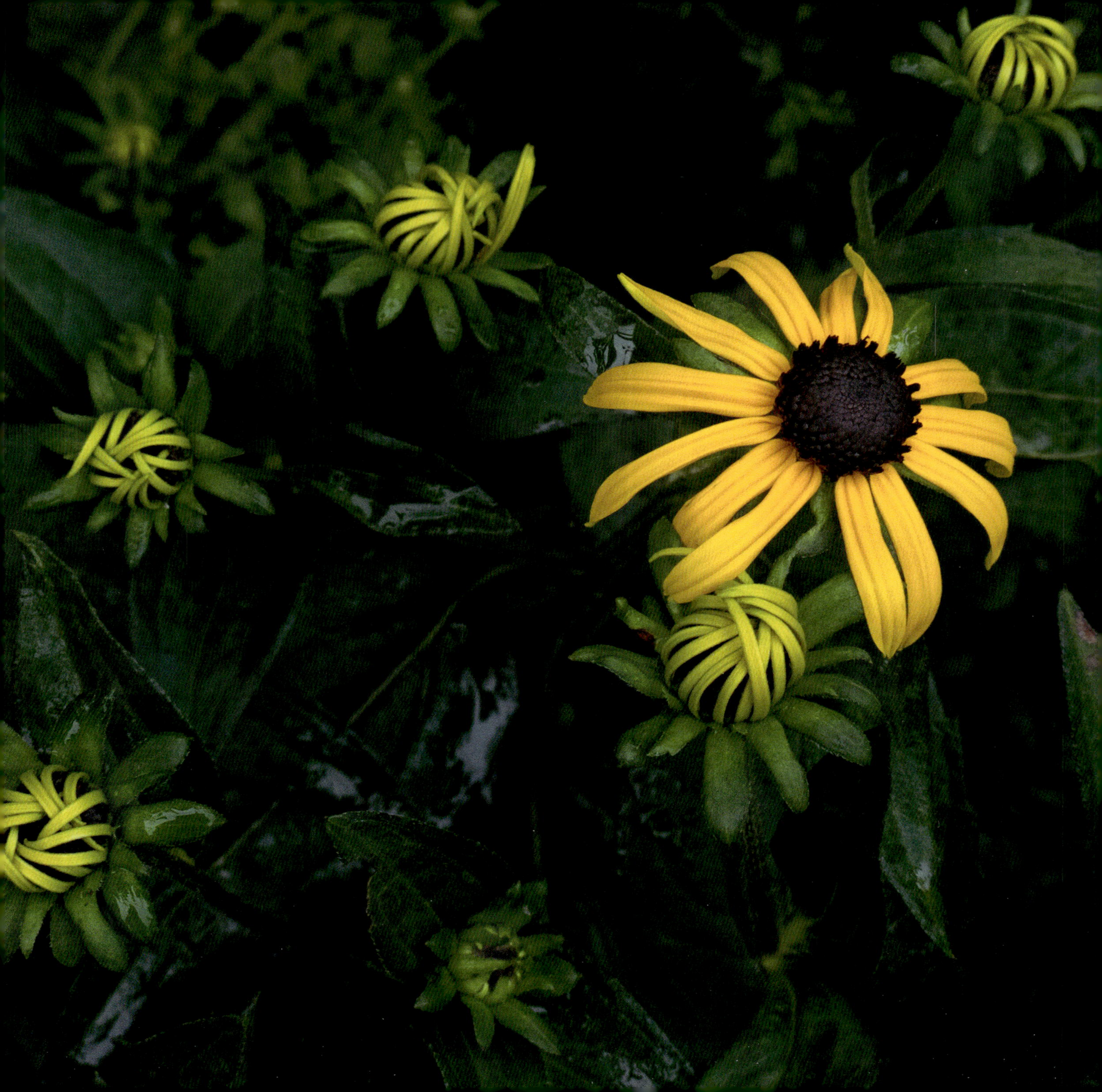

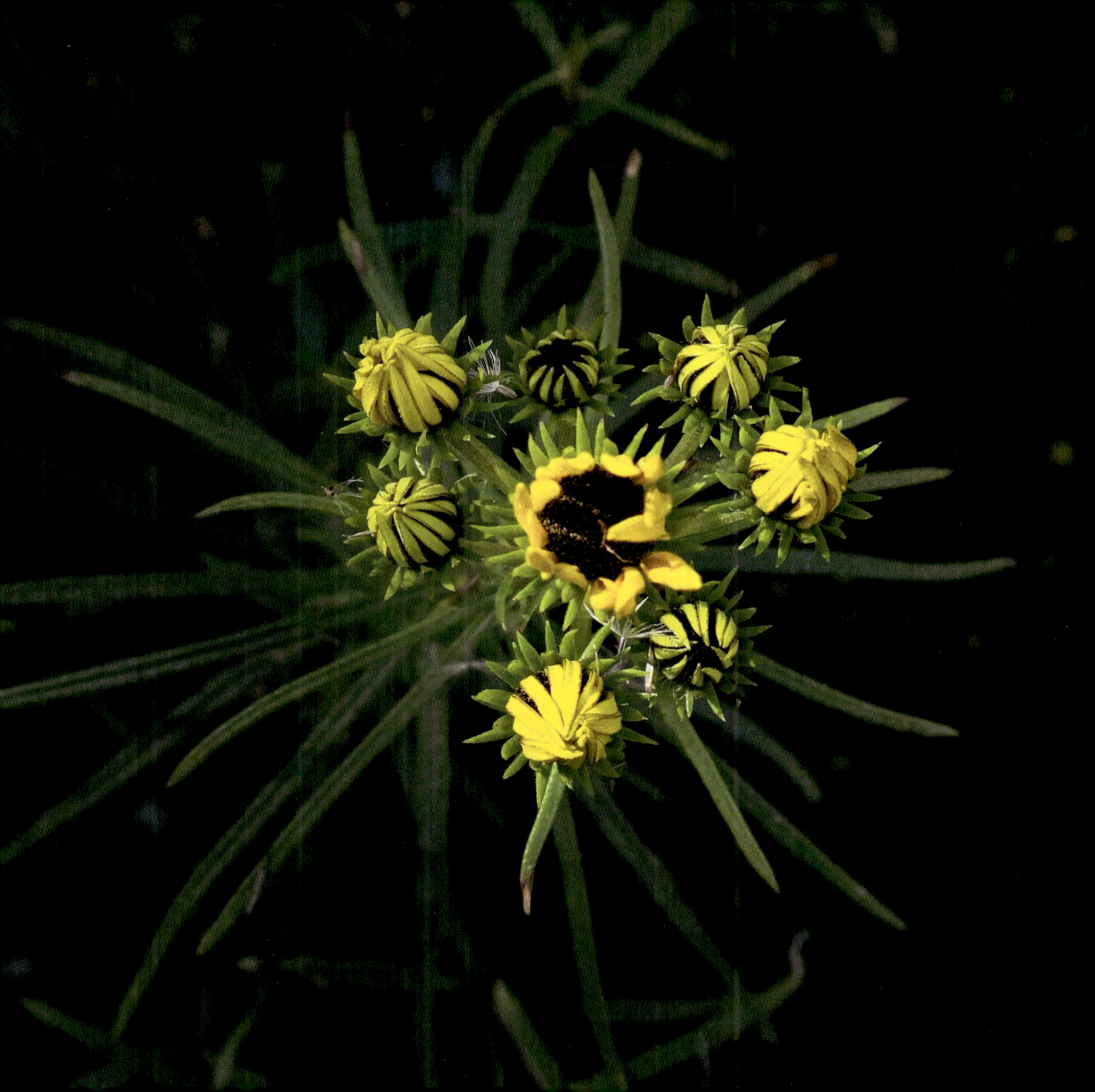

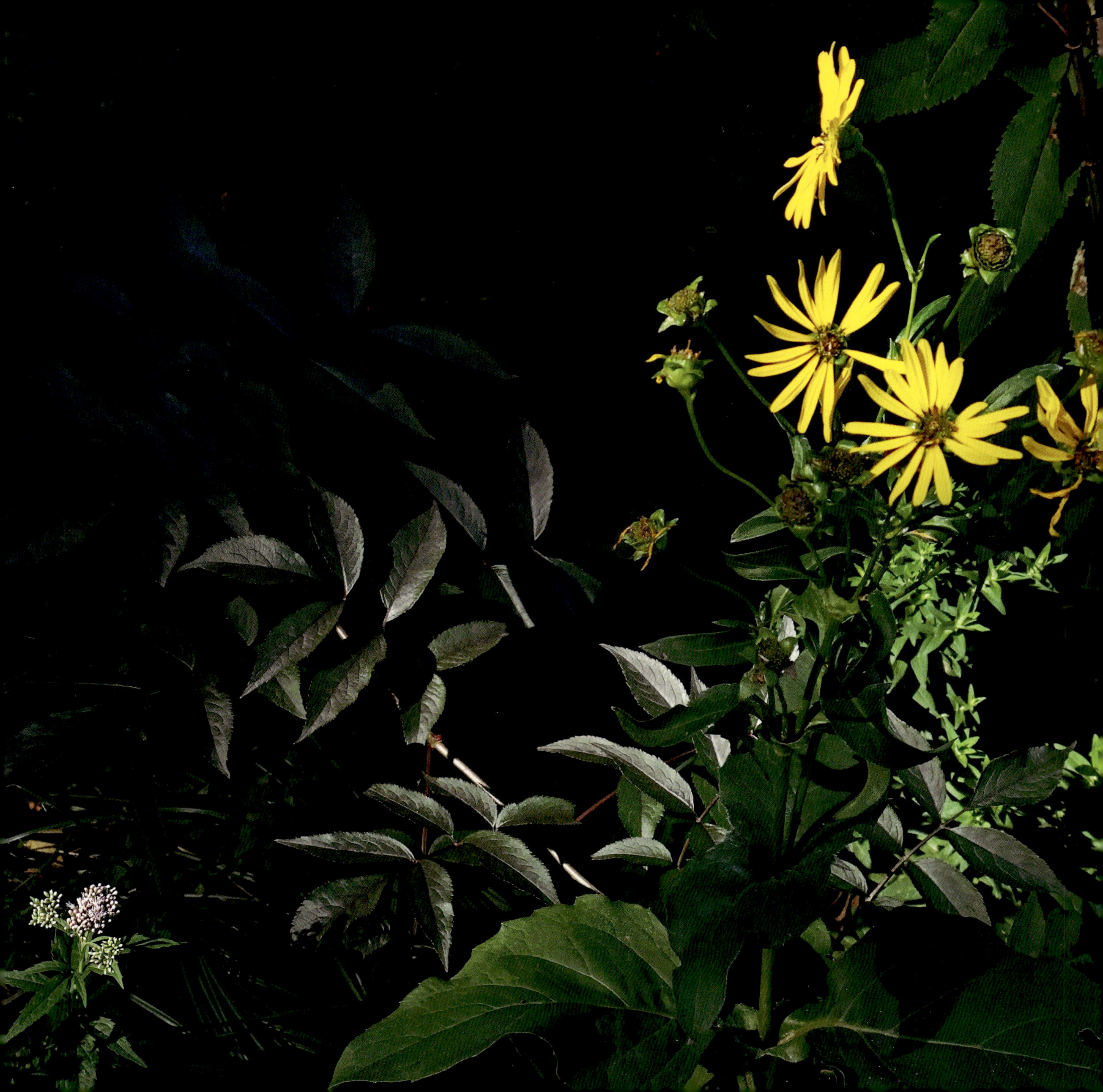

Sometimes all it takes is a single blossom.

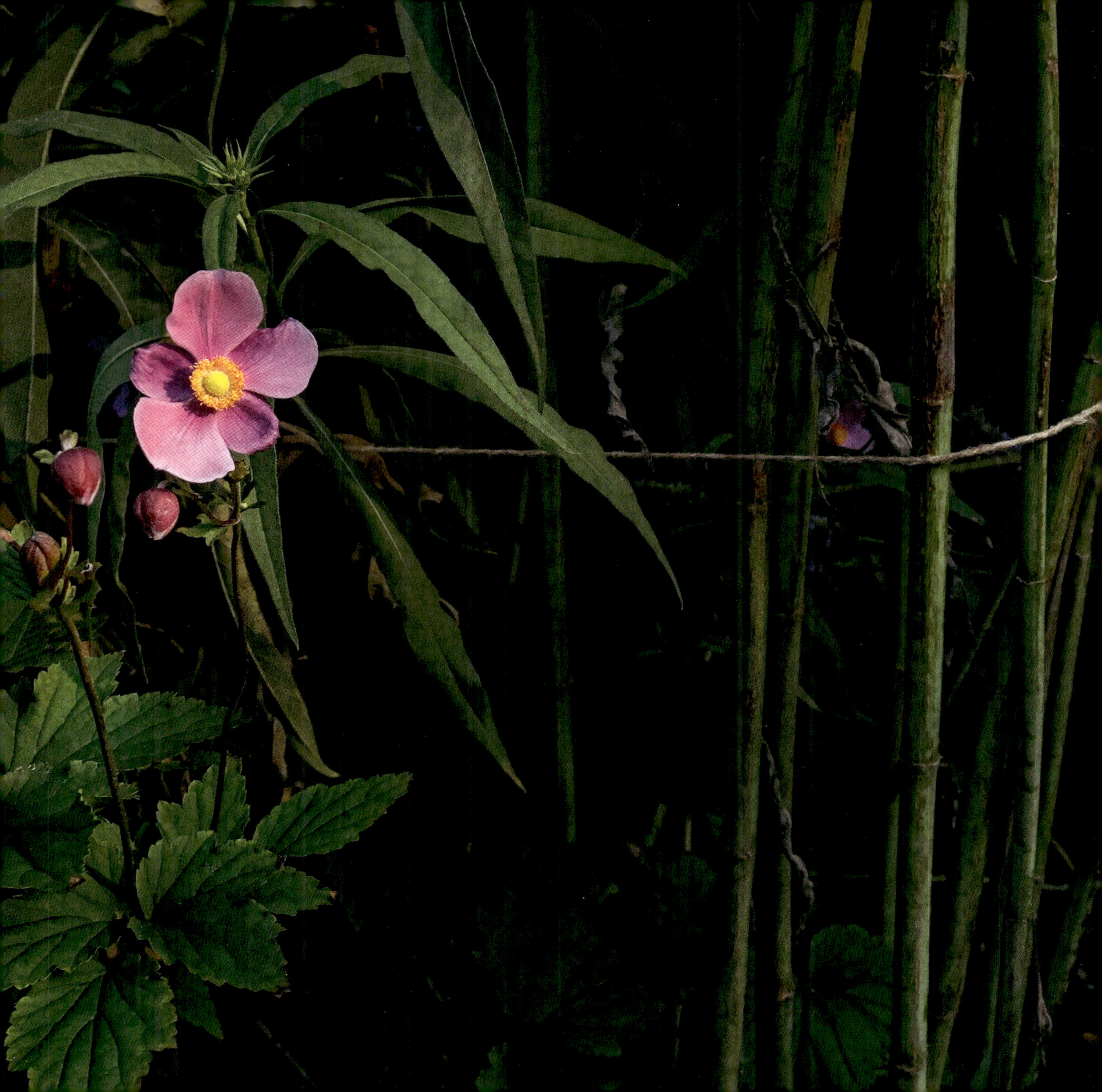

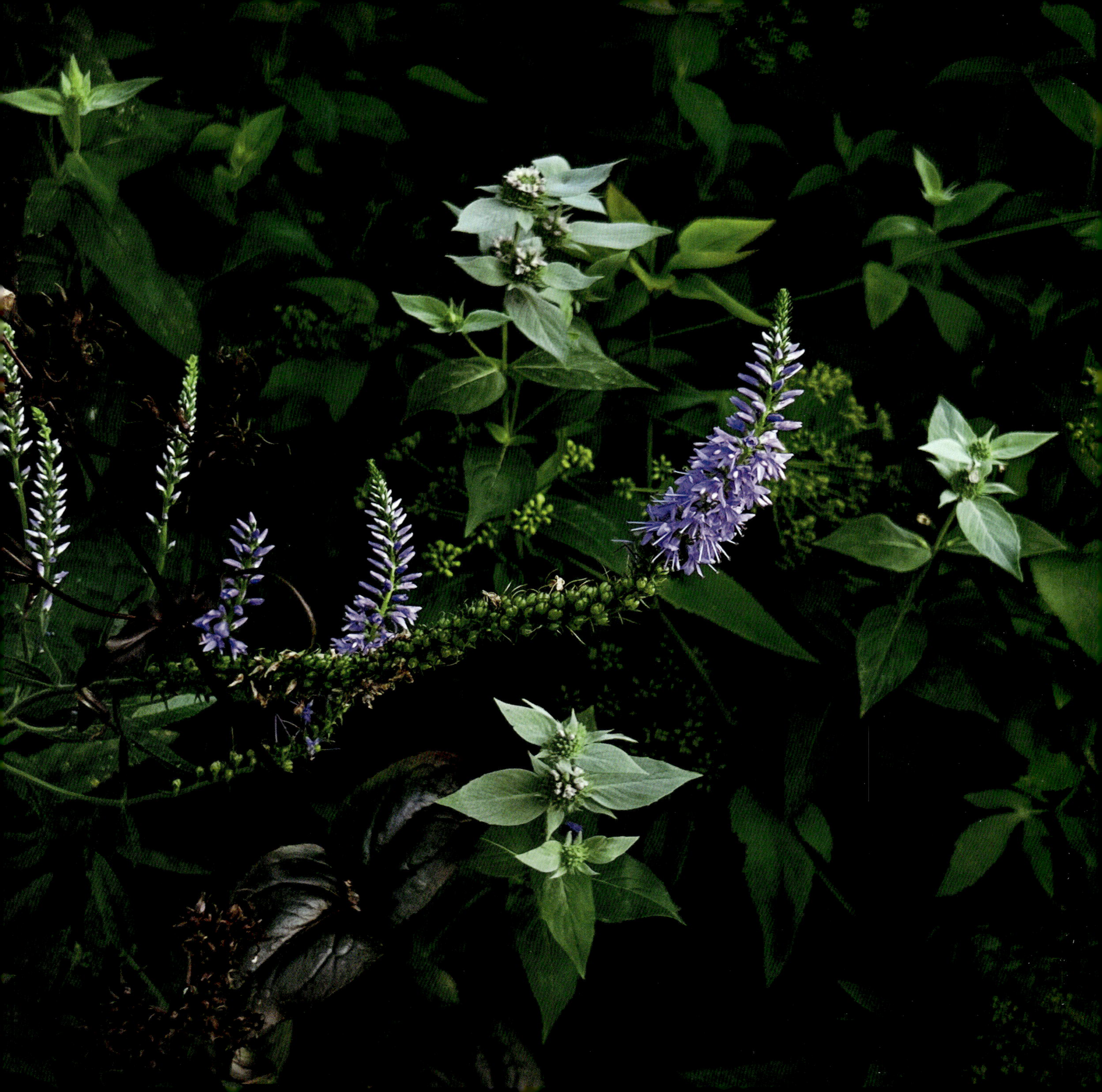

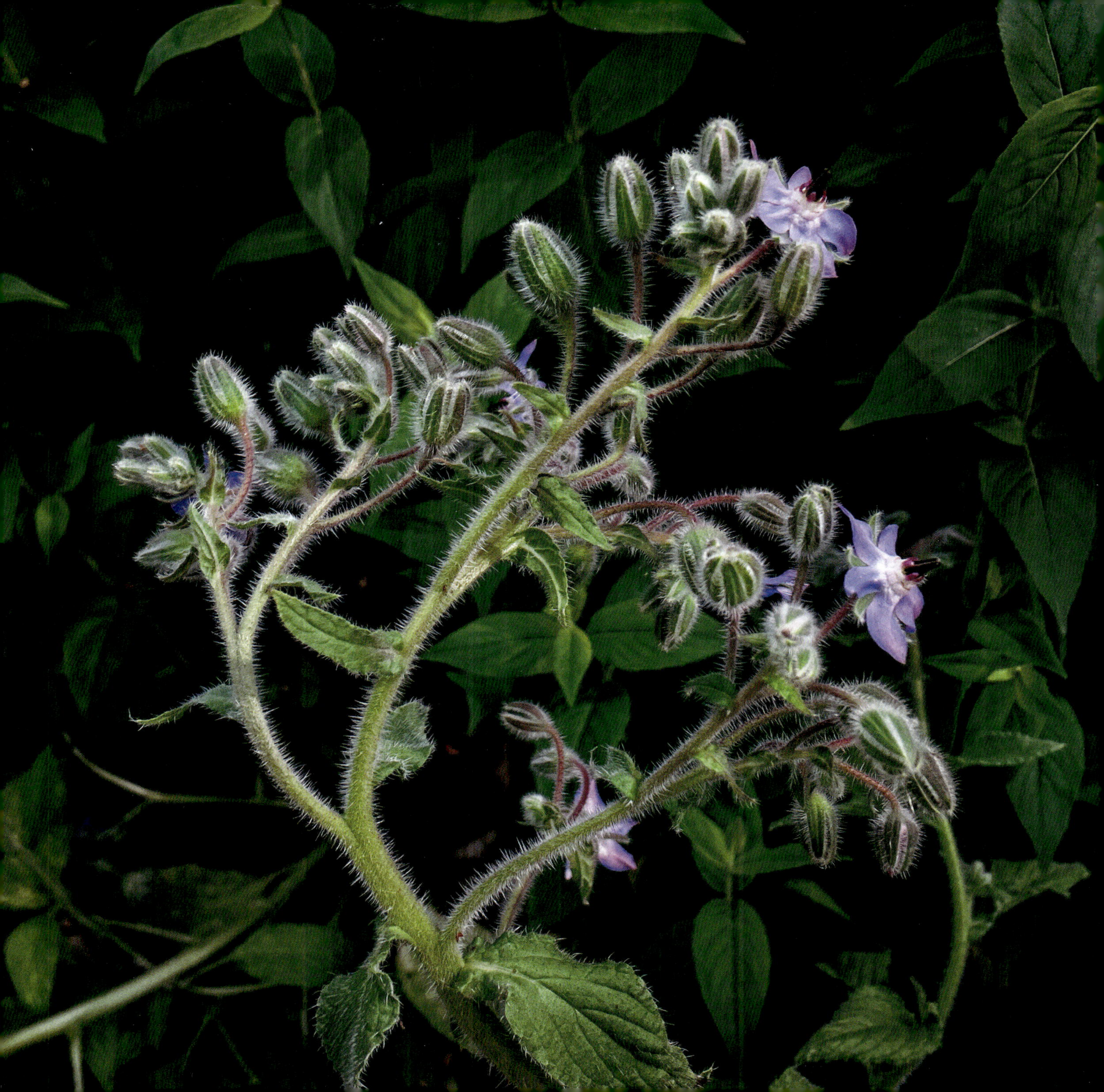

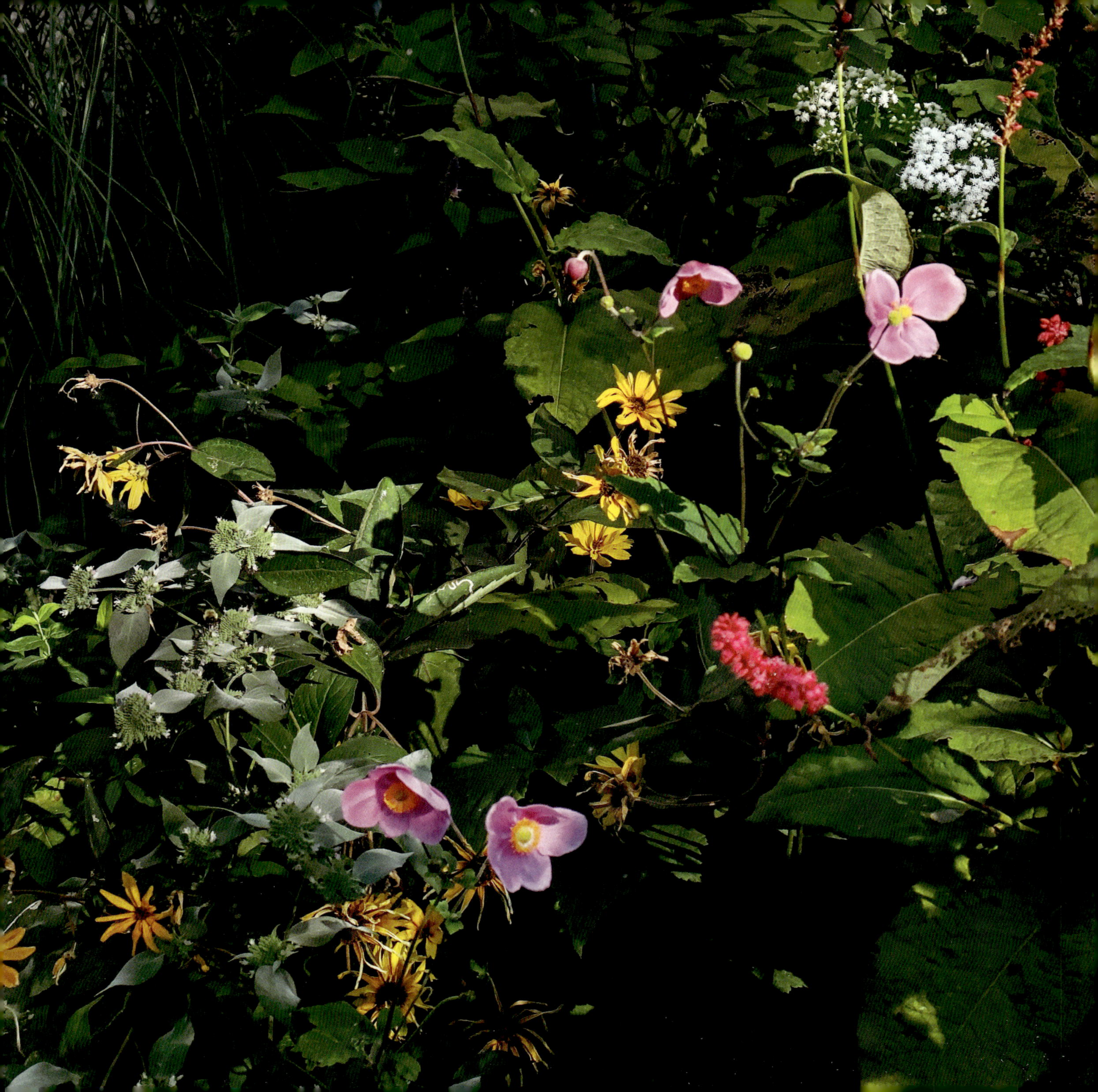

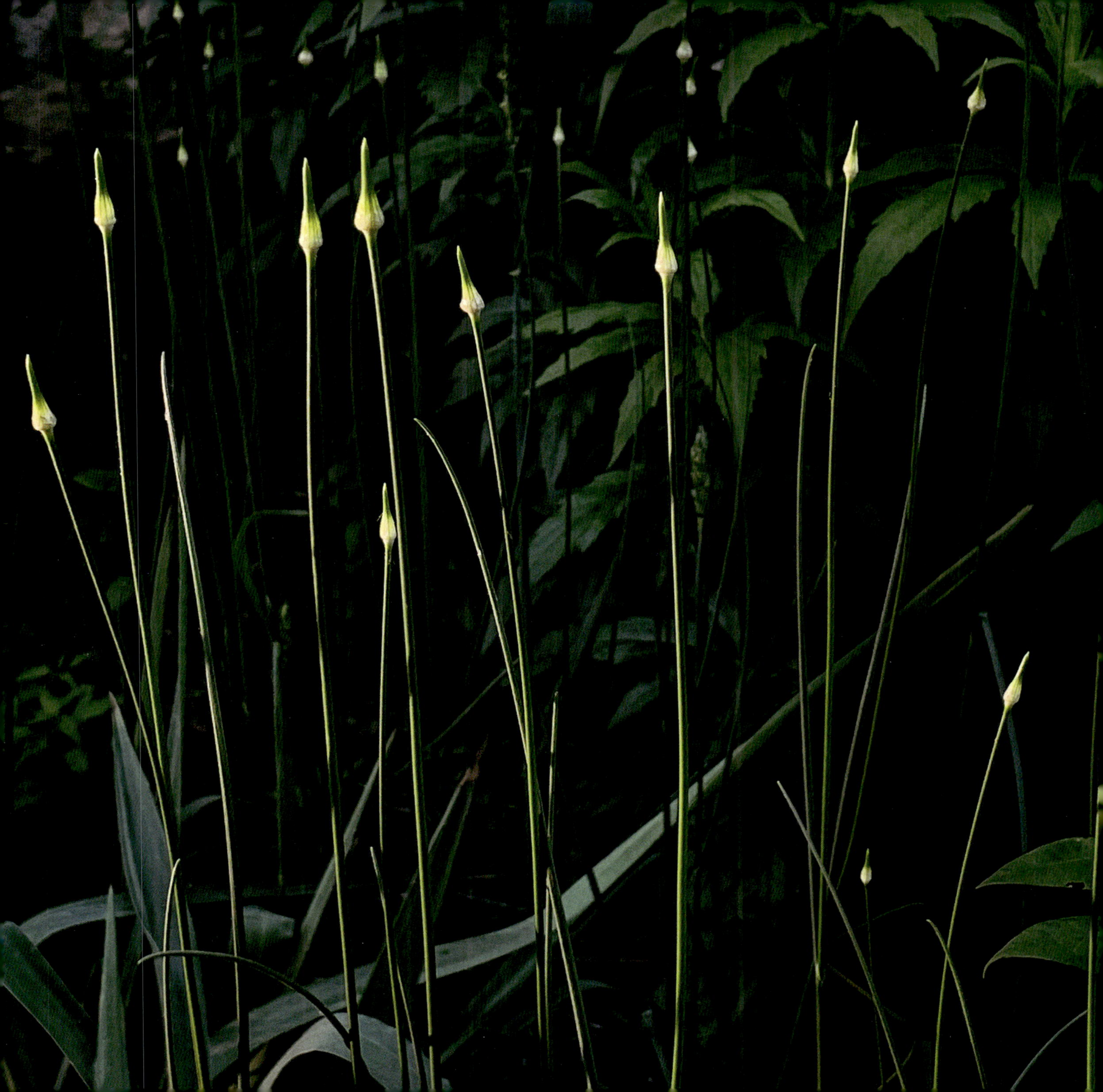

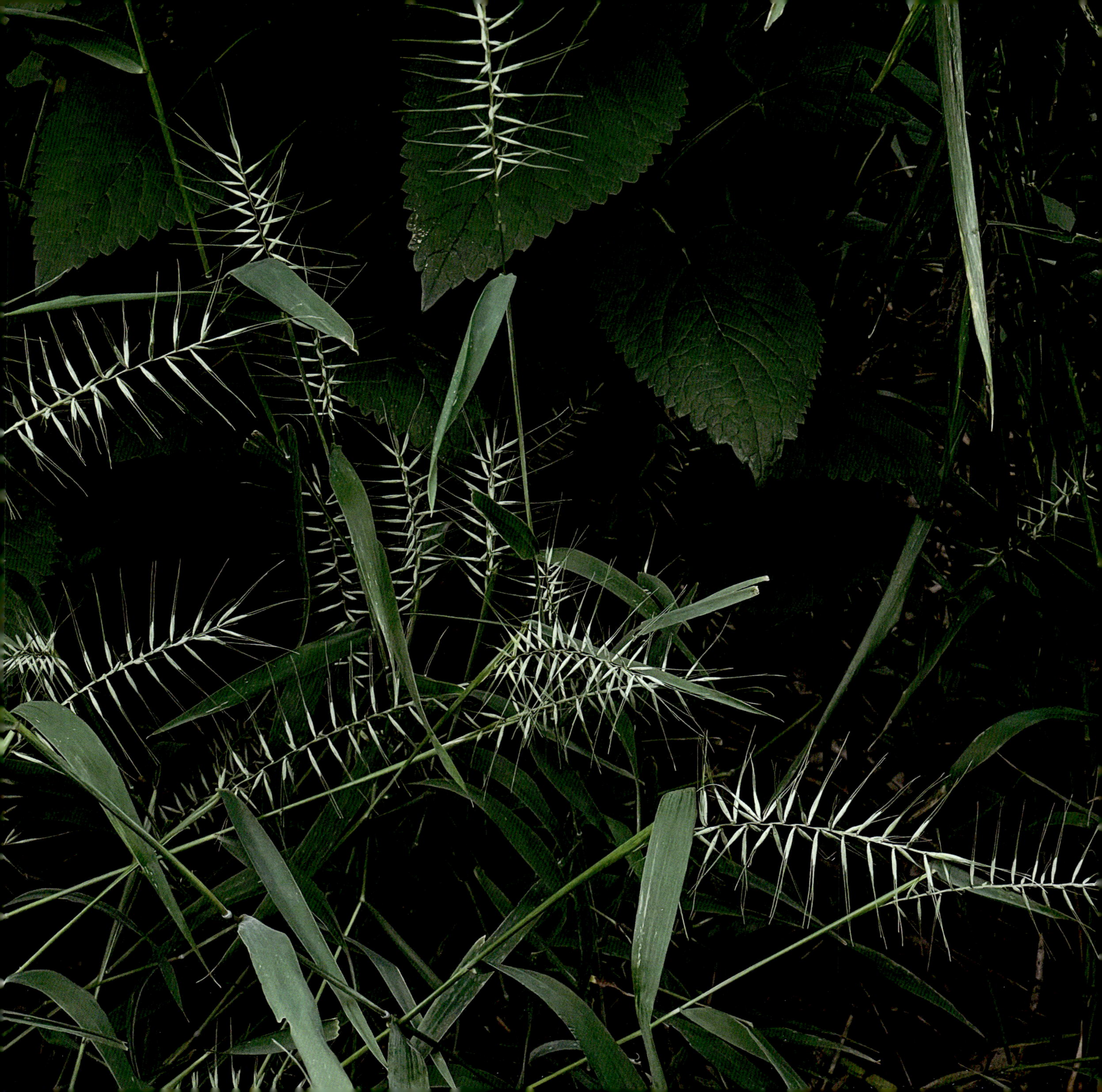

Whether I am digging in the dirt or watching how
the changing light falls on the plants,
I am in a state of peaceful connection to all of life.

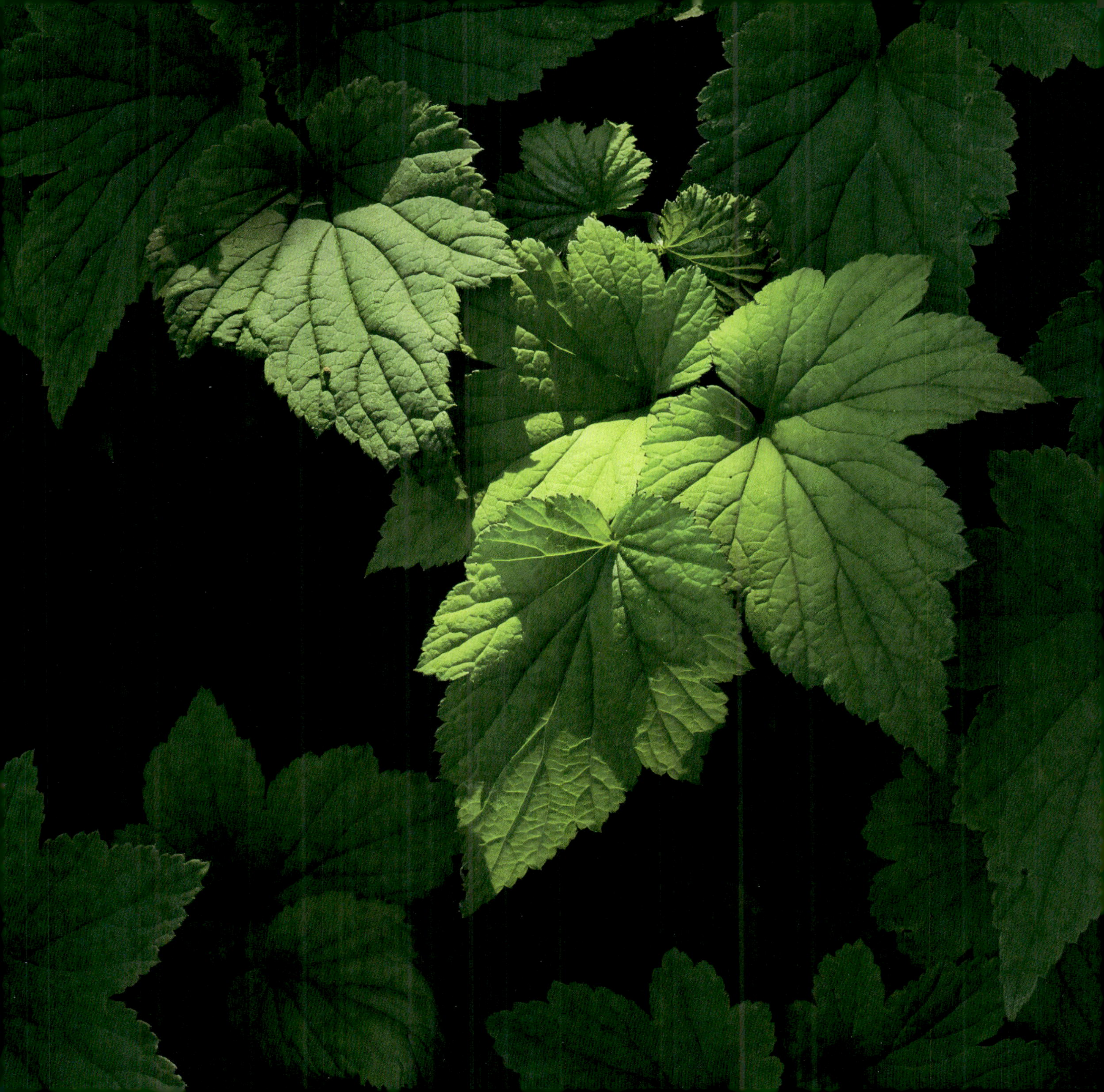

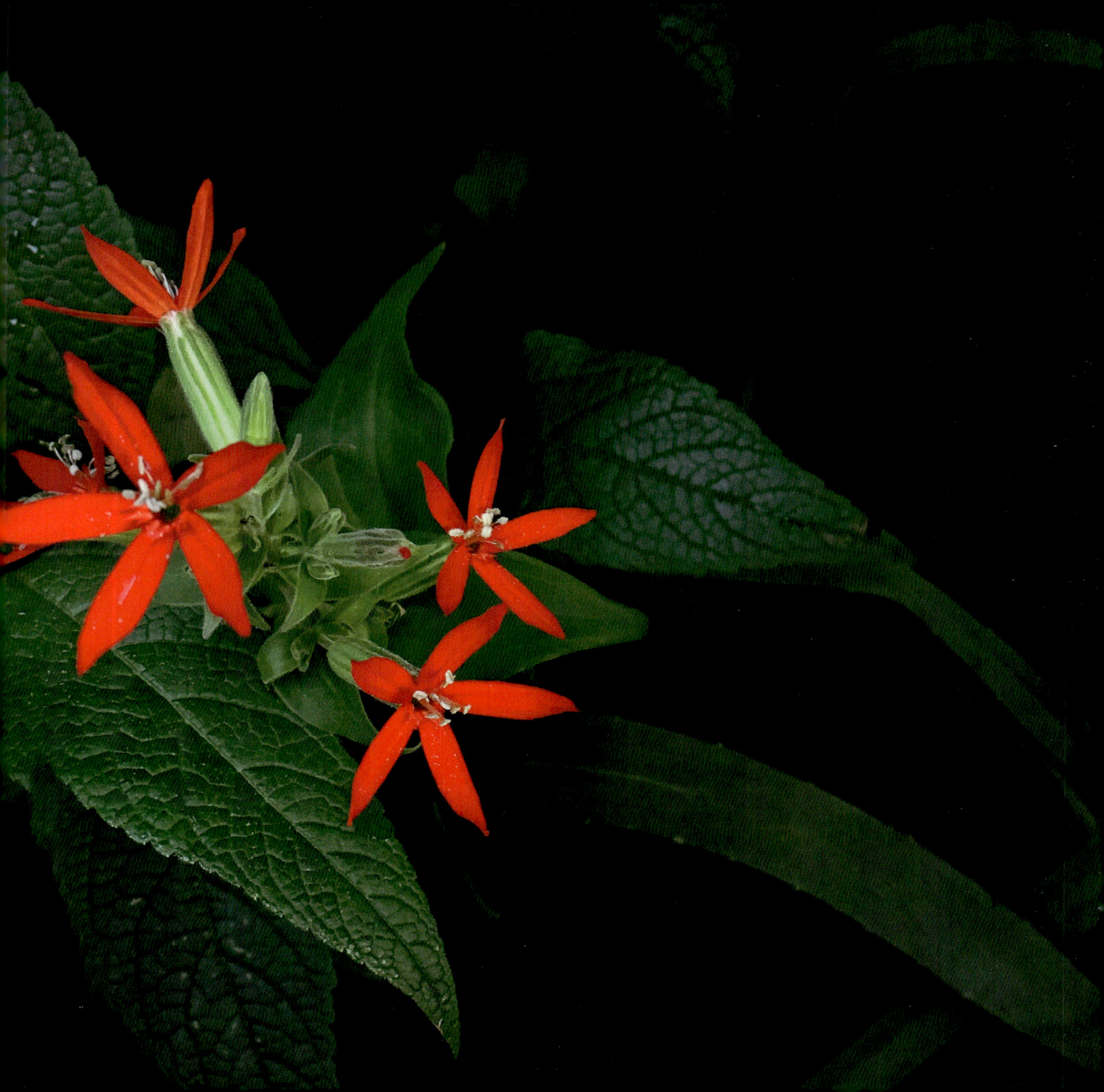

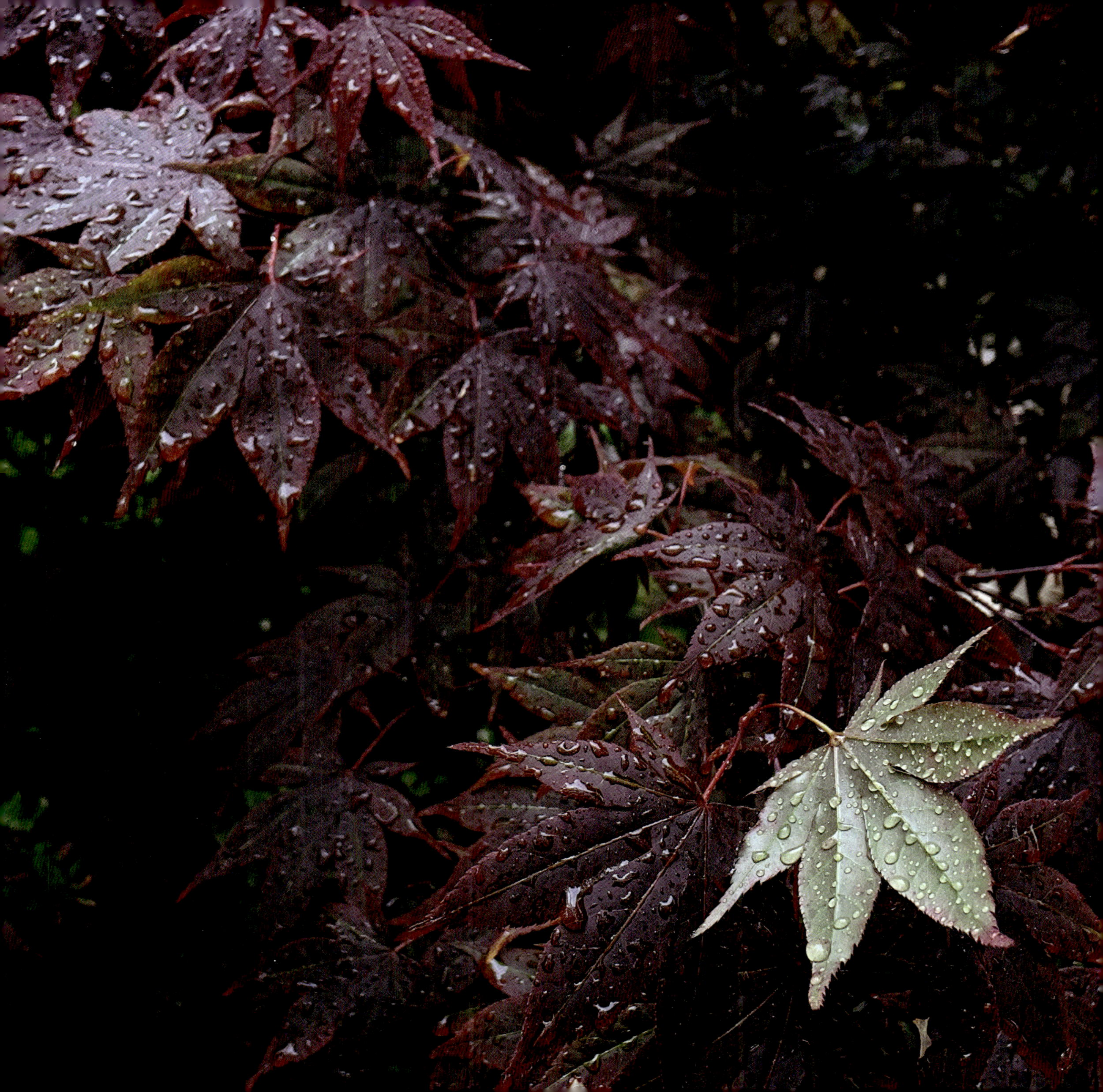

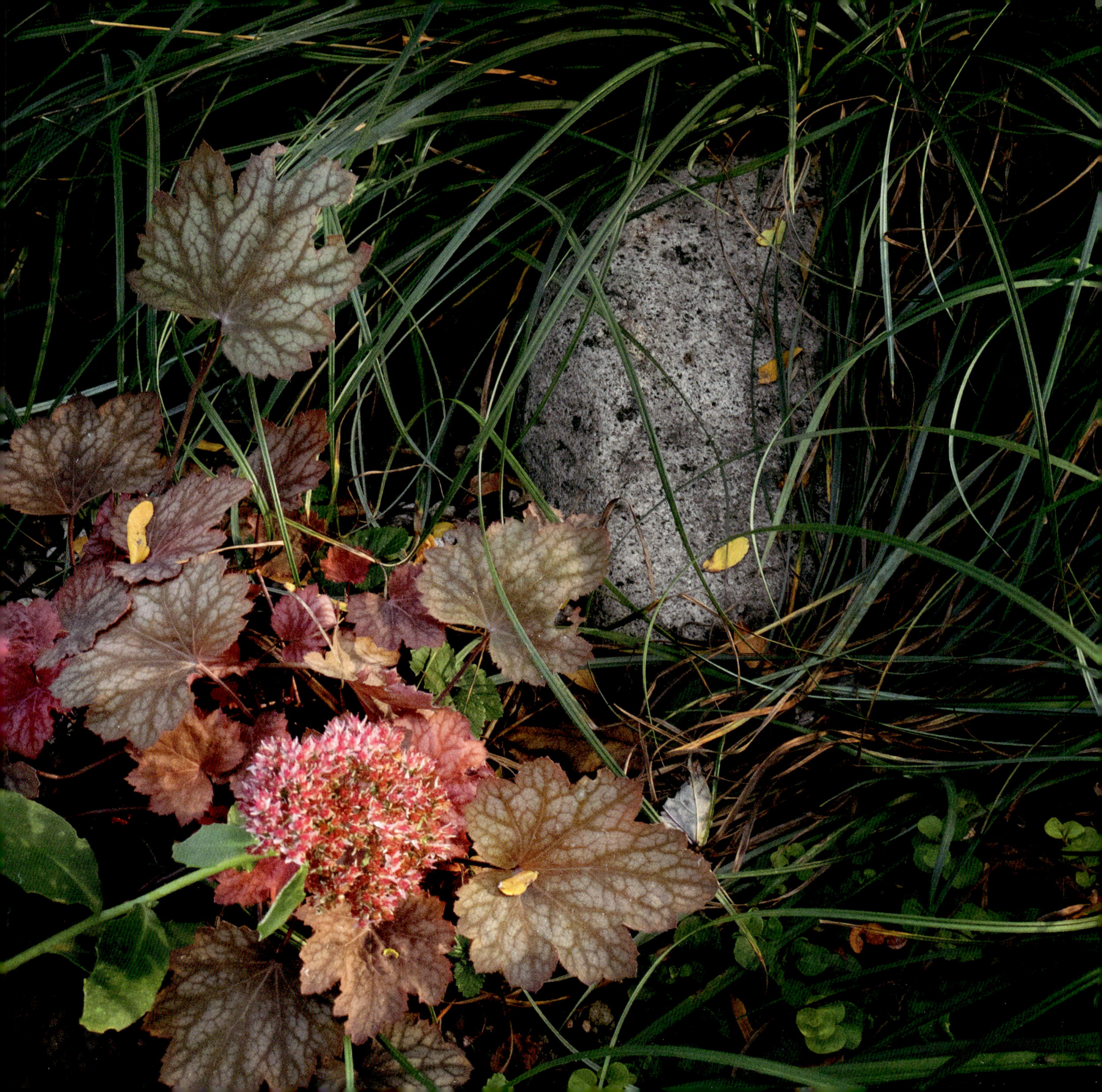

Love is another form of paying attention
and exists on many planes and in dimensions
that we do not fully understand.

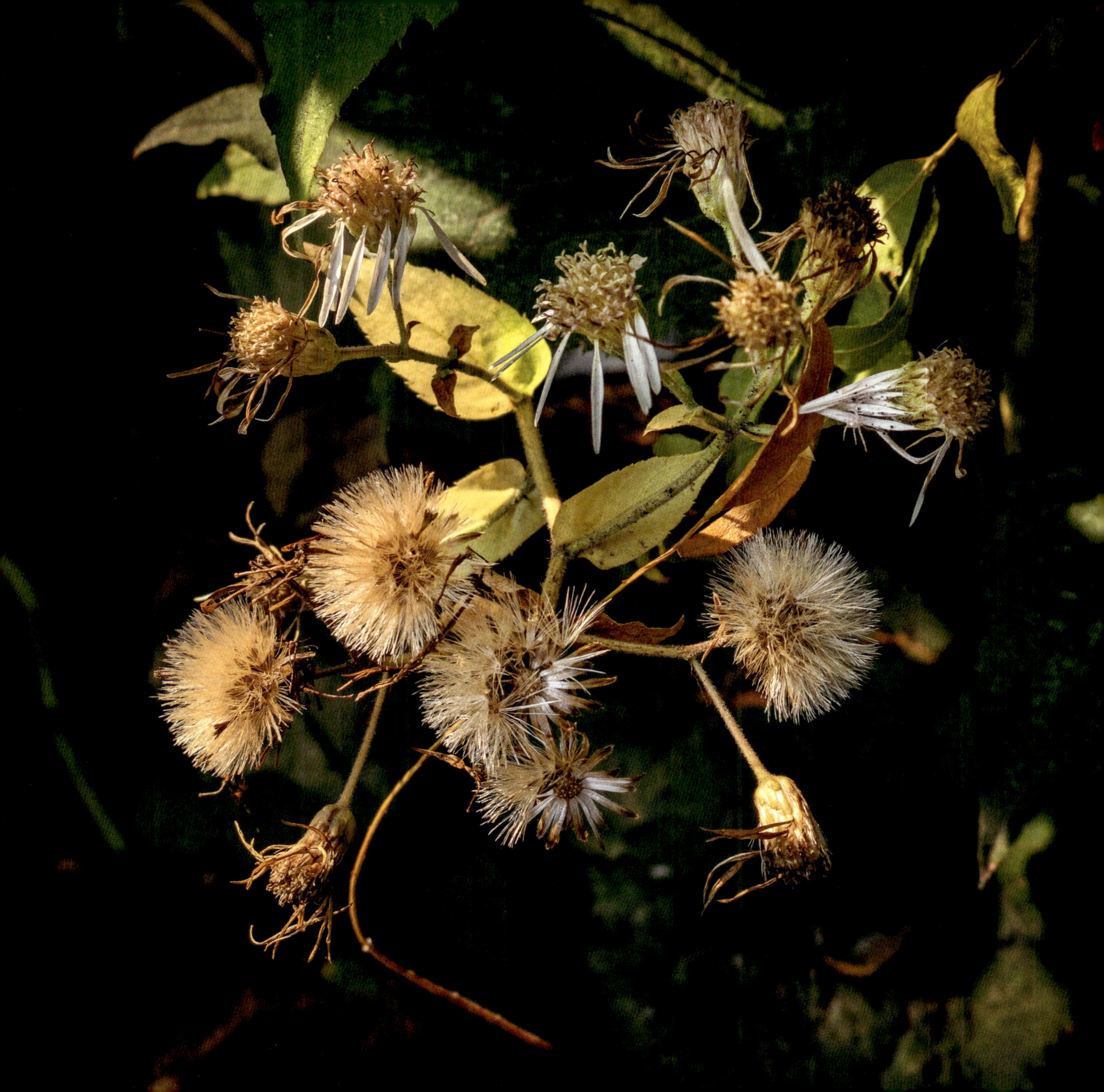

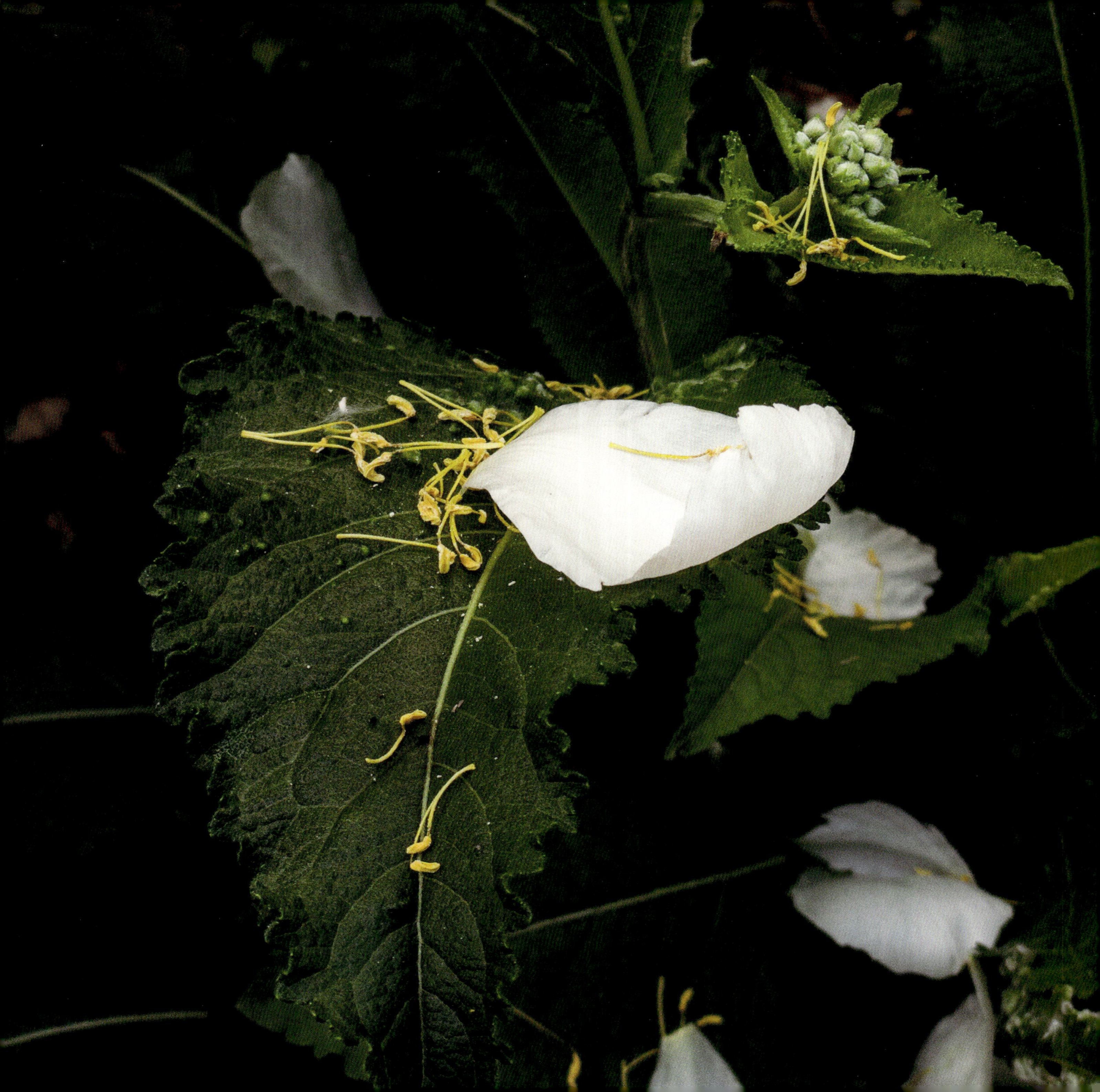

Howard's love will continue in many forms,
some of which we may not be aware.

He will continue to nurture us in life,
if we just pay attention.

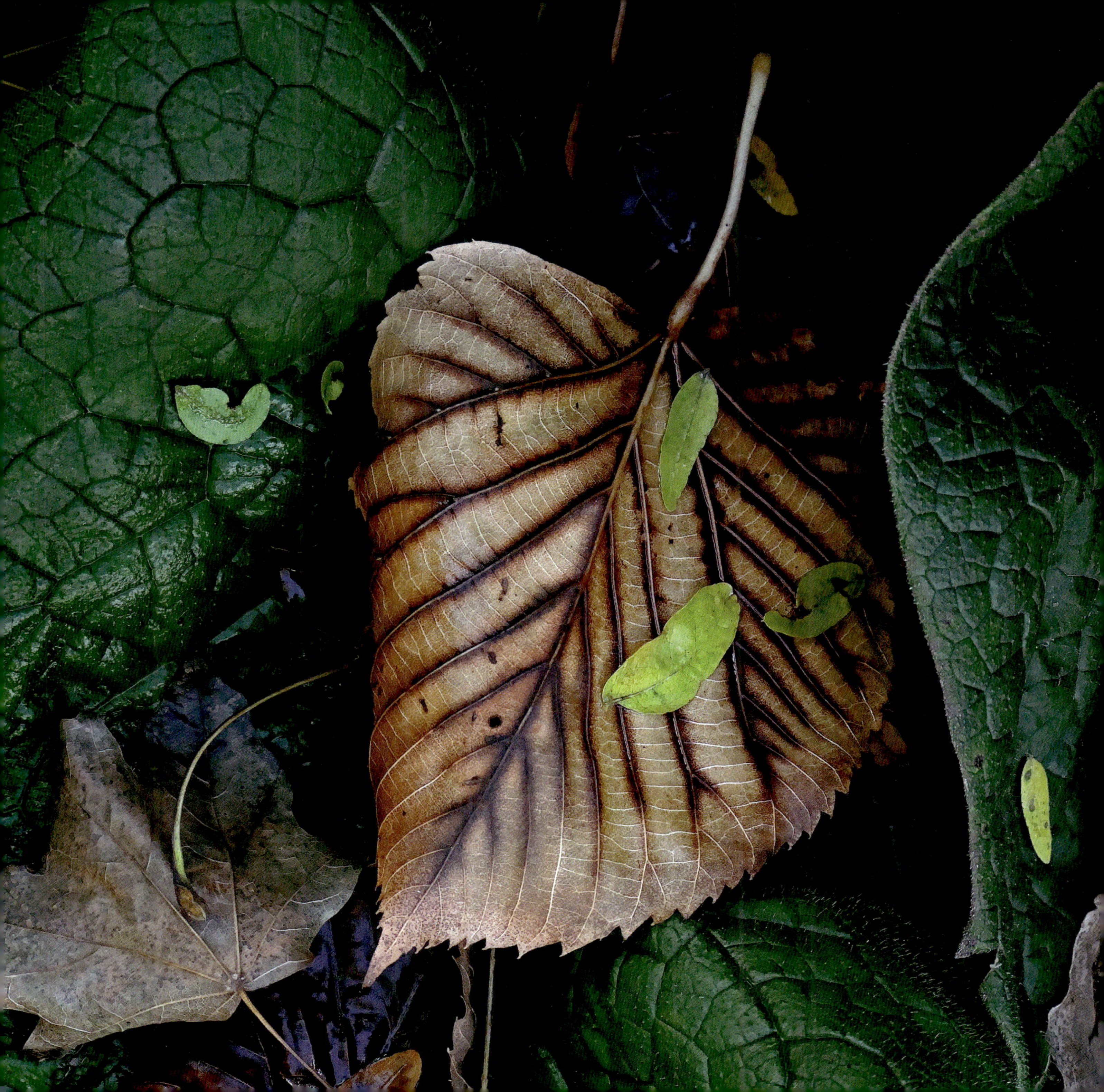

THE GREAT TRANSFORMATION

by James Baraz

There is suffering in life. This is the First Noble Truth of the Buddha's teaching. How we manage the inevitability of sorrow determines whether we see life as something to accept resignedly or as an invitation to deeply awaken to the truth of the nature of being. In opening ourselves to the pain of our loss and finding constructive ways to express all that we feel, we transform our suffering into compassion and ultimately into a more enduring kind of love. In *Still Life*, Jane Fulton Alt shows in a profound way how that transformation can be a sacred cultivation of beauty and a celebration of life.

In these stunning images, accompanied by the author's reflections, we at once feel Alt's loss and her joy as she honors her life partner's last assignment: to learn the art of gardening as a way to keep her heart open, pay tribute to the love they shared, and say "yes" to life. As she tends her husband's garden—which transforms into her own—she's tending her broken heart, allowing the sadness inside to burst forth, in its own time, into beauty and joy.

The process of grieving is mysterious. Enduring and accepting the physical loss of a loved one takes time to metabolize. The touch or living connection that had so nourished us is no more. But over time, the essence of the departed becomes ever more integrated into our being—their laughter, their joy, their goodness, the special dance of life that we shared— eventually becomes part of us. We're no longer separate. Rather, those qualities now shine through us as their legacy for everyone to enjoy.

Although no one can know another's pain, the grieving process is not a solitary journey. Psychologist and grief expert Francis Weller writes, "Grief offers a wild alchemy that transmutes suffering into fertile ground."[1] He also observes, "Grief has always been communal, always been shared and consequently has traditionally been regarded as a sacred process. Too often in modern times our grief becomes private. When our sorrows are being witnessed and held within a community of compassion, grief can surprisingly turn to joy, to a love emboldened for all that surrounds us. Love and loss have been eternally entwined. To acknowledge our grief is to free our love to fall outwards into the waiting world."[2]

In the Acknowledgments for this book, Alt appreciates the support and love that she's received from her community of dear friends and family, photography mentors, and expert gardeners who shared their knowledge and skill so generously, teaching her the secrets of cultivating beauty. Most of all, she's been accompanied by the living beings that have blossomed magnificently under her care. Tending to these exquisite expressions of life, it seems that Nature herself has become Alt's greatest companion and comforter as she starts healing the loneliness and dissolving the feelings of separation. In bringing the garden back to life, she is Nature taking care of itself.

Spiritual teacher Ekhart Tolle describes how flowers are evidence of the divine benevolence of life. Life didn't have to create beauty to exist. It is a gratuitous gift for all to enjoy. Tolle makes the case for flowers playing an essential part in the evolution of our consciousness. We are drawn to and fascinated by them. He writes that seeing beauty in a flower awakens us to the beauty that is an essential part of our own innermost being, our true nature.

In *Still Life*, we witness how sorrow can give birth to beauty and how loss can lead to a deeper connection with life. Jane Fulton Alt invites us to see the inevitable suffering that comes our way as an opportunity to not only heal from our grieving but to use it as a means of deepening our love and appreciation for being alive. I hope you enjoy this book as much as I have and that it helps you, too, feel the blessing and mystery of life.

Endnotes
1. Francis Weller, *The Wild Edge of Sorrow: Rituals of Renewal and the Sacred Work of Grief* (Berkeley, CA: North Atlantic Books, 2015), p. 8.
2. Francis Weller, email correspondence with author, November 10, 2025.

Gardening for the Future

by Douglas Tallamy

Most of us think very little about what lies ahead. The frenetic business of our daily lives and the days and weeks immediately before us usually block our ability to visualize the more distant future. And if we do try to imagine it, our vision is almost always blurry at best. For a growing number of lucky souls, though, that vision is coming into sharper focus, and for a very few it has become crystal clear. No longer will we segregate nature from the human experience. No longer will we incarcerate the natural world on uninhabitable mountaintops or unbuildable wetlands. No longer will we treat the living things around us as interesting but inessential curios, as if we didn't depend on them in the same way an infant depends upon its mother. In the very near future, humanity will coexist with nature—where we live, work, play, and farm.

I know this, and Howard Alt knew this, because it is the only sustainable path forward.

Since 2004 I have been talking and writing about the need to coexist with nature rather than exiling it to scattered parks and preserves that are too small, too isolated, and too few to sustain the species that run the ecosystems that support us. These preserves are not working, for if they were, we would not be experiencing the planet's sixth great extinction event; we would not have lost three billion breeding North American birds in the last fifty years; we would not be reading headlines about global insect declines; and the United Nations would not be predicting the extinction of a million species in the next twenty years. If we humans are to establish a sustainable relationship with the natural world—the world we rely on—we will have to practice serious conservation outside of our parks and preserves. I have said all these things many times, but talk is cheap.

It will require action by many to reshape the way we landscape to enhance ecosystem function rather than degrade it. This is exactly the type of action Howard took shortly before his death.

Our new relationship with nature must be collaborative. Western and Asian cultures have pursued an adversarial relationship with the natural world for centuries, not out of necessity but for convenience. We have largely achieved this convenience, but it has come with an enormous price tag: the destruction of our life support systems. To function sustainably, all landscapes need to sequester carbon, support diverse communities of pollinators, employ the native plants that sustain the food webs that drive local ecosystems, and manage the watersheds in which they lay. By reducing the area in lawn and artfully deploying ecologically productive native plants, new-age gardeners, like Howard was, are designing and implementing landscapes that do all those things and more. And as more people adopt Howard's vision, biological corridors that help connect existing wildlands with each other will take shape across the landscape, enabling those wild areas to more effectively protect the biodiversity within.

As Howard discovered, there are a number of ecological advantages associated with conservation landscaping. By using many more plants, especially trees, than are found in our current landscapes, we can pull carbon dioxide out of the atmosphere and thus help fight climate change. One-third of the carbon in the atmosphere has come from removing plants from planet Earth in recent millennia.

Well-planted landscapes—those with less lawn—also directly address watershed problems by encouraging infiltration, reducing stormwater runoff, removing pollutants before they enter watersheds, and reducing the use of unnecessary fertilizers and pesticides. Landscapes designed with ecologically powerful native plants will reduce the use of invasive ornamentals such as burning bush, Callery pear, Oriental bittersweet, autumn olive, porcelain berry, privet, Norway maple, Zelkova, and many more non-native plants that have become tumors in our North American natural areas.

Our only home is facing two enormous environmental crises: climate change and the loss of biodiversity. Grassroots actions like Howard's are addressing both simultaneously. The future of conservation lies in landscaping that includes, rather than excludes, nature outside of our parks and preserves.

Howard Alt not only understood this but was also an early leader in implementing such conservation. Fortunately for everyone, and for the natural world itself, Howard's approach to landscaping lives on after him.

ILLUMINATION

by W. M. Hunt

"How can we manage to illuminate the pathos of our lives?"

— Jorge Luis Borges

Think of the title *Still Life* as in: there is still life to live. Life continues. It has not been stilled or stopped.

This garden of Jane Fulton Alt's flora is intense. As Alt takes us through her garden, the darkness gives the work intention; it helps us to see. It is quiet—the heat of the sun has cooled, and the daytime frenzy of insects and birds feeding has stilled. We can make our way through this part of the world and the artist's head, calmly, with some stealth. Shhh. Is this real or imagined?

The word "illuminate" as both verb and noun describes the artist. She seeks light and enlightenment. She has a luminous soul. She wants intellectual and spiritual clarity. There is tenderness here, not despair. Sadness yes, but not anguish. The artist is passing through, feeling her way. Processing.

Alt is in search of transcendence. We all are. What is unique to her is that she lives in various dimensions of transcendence simultaneously and visits our earthly realm periodically, though often enough that no one reports her missing. She seems like the most grounded soul in the world, but she is scudding through the clouds.

Another word to describe her is fecund. Alt has children and grandchildren, but for this discussion, it is her imagination and way of seeing that are fertile. Her garden is vital. She brings patience to her time in the garden so that she can truly discover its contents, and by extension, show that to us.

Looking at these photographs gives us the impression that Alt has looked at and remembered the works of great American still life painters like Martin Johnson Heade or Raphaelle Peale, which transcend their trompe l'oeil brilliance. Georgia O'Keefe was an important artist also in search of the sublime. There is some Henri Rousseau jungle in these pictures too. Alt knows her history of art.

She brings her distinct way of searching, seeing.

Alt's colors are deep and intense. She also likes surface—the way light travels along an edge or stem, how the color modulates subtly, depending on the intensity of the illumination. She appreciates line, the ins and outs of petals overlapping, leaves folding in on themselves. She goes to the garden, or she sets flowers on the table, laying them out artfully like lab specimens, as if she were the great-granddaughter of Karl Blossfeldt, here in color, just as deliberate but less dry and driven.

Alt's late husband, Howard, is at the center of her story. Theirs was by all accounts a great romance and collaboration, brought to life charmingly in this sweet dance of red ranunculus. Howard was the gardener, and he left it to Jane to cultivate the garden and discover its treasures.

In the final scenes of *King Lear*, the mad king encounters the blinded Gloucester and bleakly offers, "yet you see how this world goes." Gloucester responds, "I see it feelingly."

Jane Fulton Alt is our guide to this secret garden, a place of healing and still living.

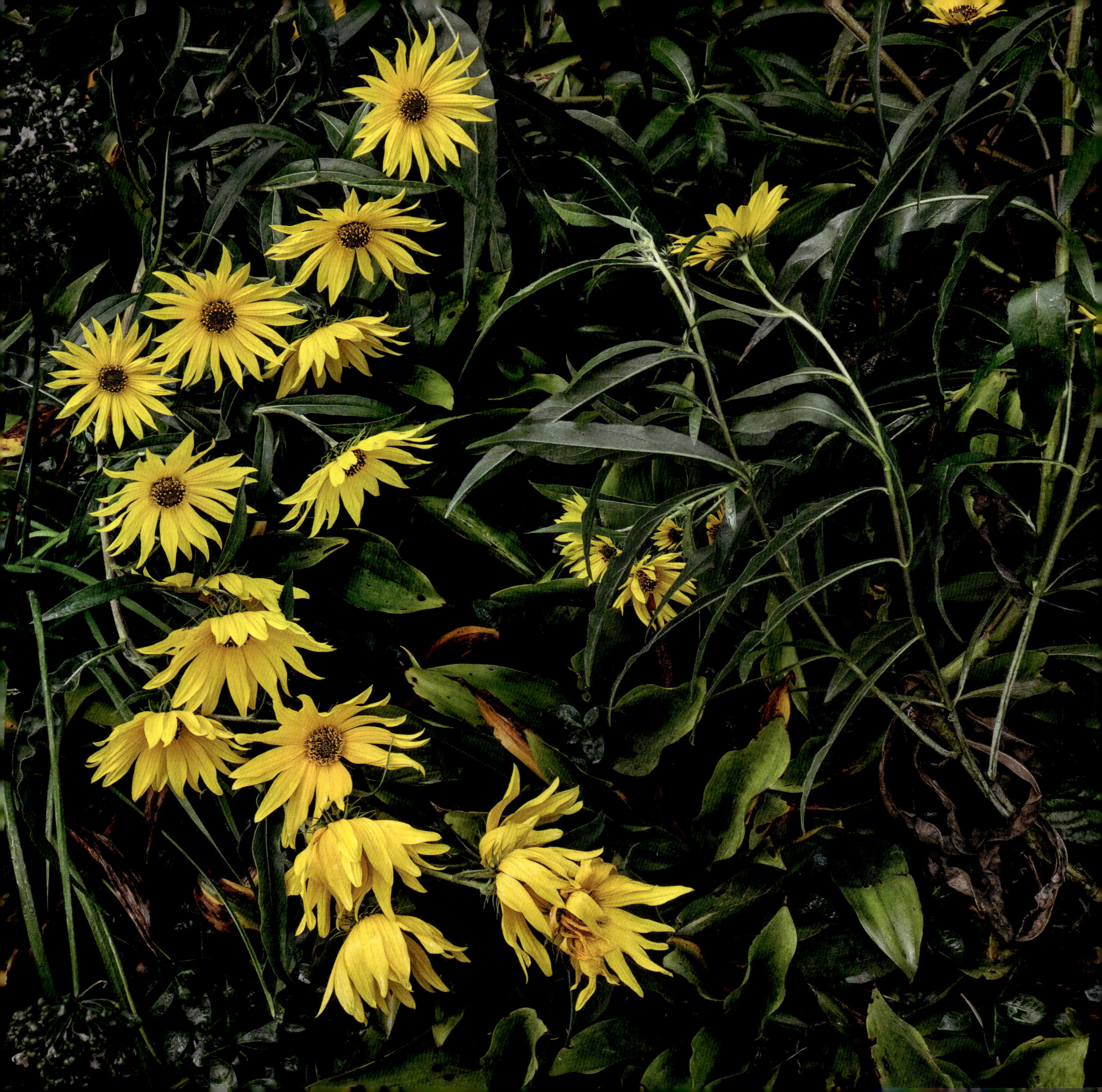

About the Author

Jane Fulton Alt was born in Chicago in 1951 and began exploring the visual arts while pursuing a career as a clinical social worker. Her award-winning photography explores the universality of the human condition and the non-material world. Alt received a BA from the University of Michigan and an MA from the University of Chicago. She studied at the Evanston Art Center, as well as at Columbia College and the Art Institute of Chicago. Alt is the author of *Look and Leave: Photographs and Stories from New Orleans's Lower Ninth Ward* (2009) and *The Burn* (2013). Her portfolio "Crude Awakening" appeared in publications worldwide.

Alt's work is held in thirty-one permanent and private collections, including Smithsonian National Museum of American History, Washington, D.C.; Museum of Fine Arts, Houston; Sunnhordland Museum, Stord, Norway; Niigata Science Museum, Japan; Museum of Contemporary Photography, Chicago; and New Orleans Museum of Art. Her work is in many special library collections, including Savannah College of Art and Design, UCLA, University of Illinois, University of Vermont, University of Washington, Wesleyan University, and Yale University. She is the recipient of numerous awards and artist residencies.

Alt resides in Evanston, Illinois, and her beloved adopted city, New Orleans.

Contributors

James Baraz
James Baraz is a founding teacher of Spirit Rock Meditation Center and has led the online course "Awakening Joy" since 2003. He serves as a guiding teacher to One Earth Sangha, a virtual "EcoDharma" center devoted to Buddhist responses to climate change. He is the co-author of *Awakening Joy* (2012) and *Awakening Joy for Kids* (2016).

Douglas Tallamy
Douglas Tallamy is a Professor of Agriculture at the University of Delaware, where he has authored more than one hundred research publications and has taught insect-related courses for more than forty-five years. Chief among his research goals is to better understand the many ways insects interact with plants and how such interactions determine the diversity of animal communities. His work has transformed our understanding of the relationship between native plants and wildlife. He is the author of *Bringing Nature Home* (2007), *The Living Landscape*, co-authored with Rick Darke (2014), *Nature's Best Hope*, a *New York Times* bestseller (2020), and *The Nature of Oaks* (2021).

W. M. Hunt
W. M. "Bill" Hunt is a champion of photography: a collector, curator, and consultant who lives and works in New York City. Hunt has been looking at and talking about photography for many years. Photography changed his life. It gave him one.

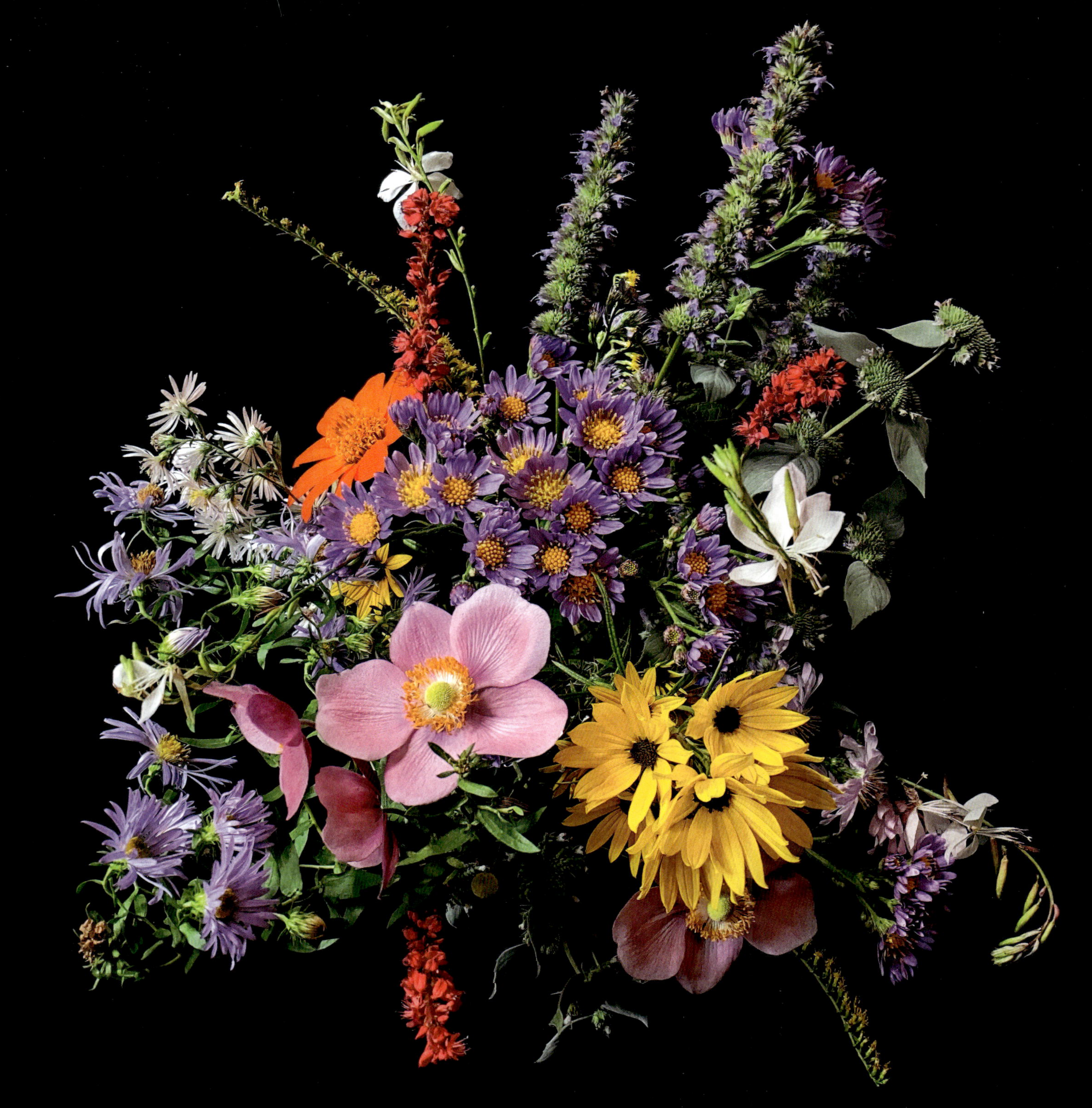

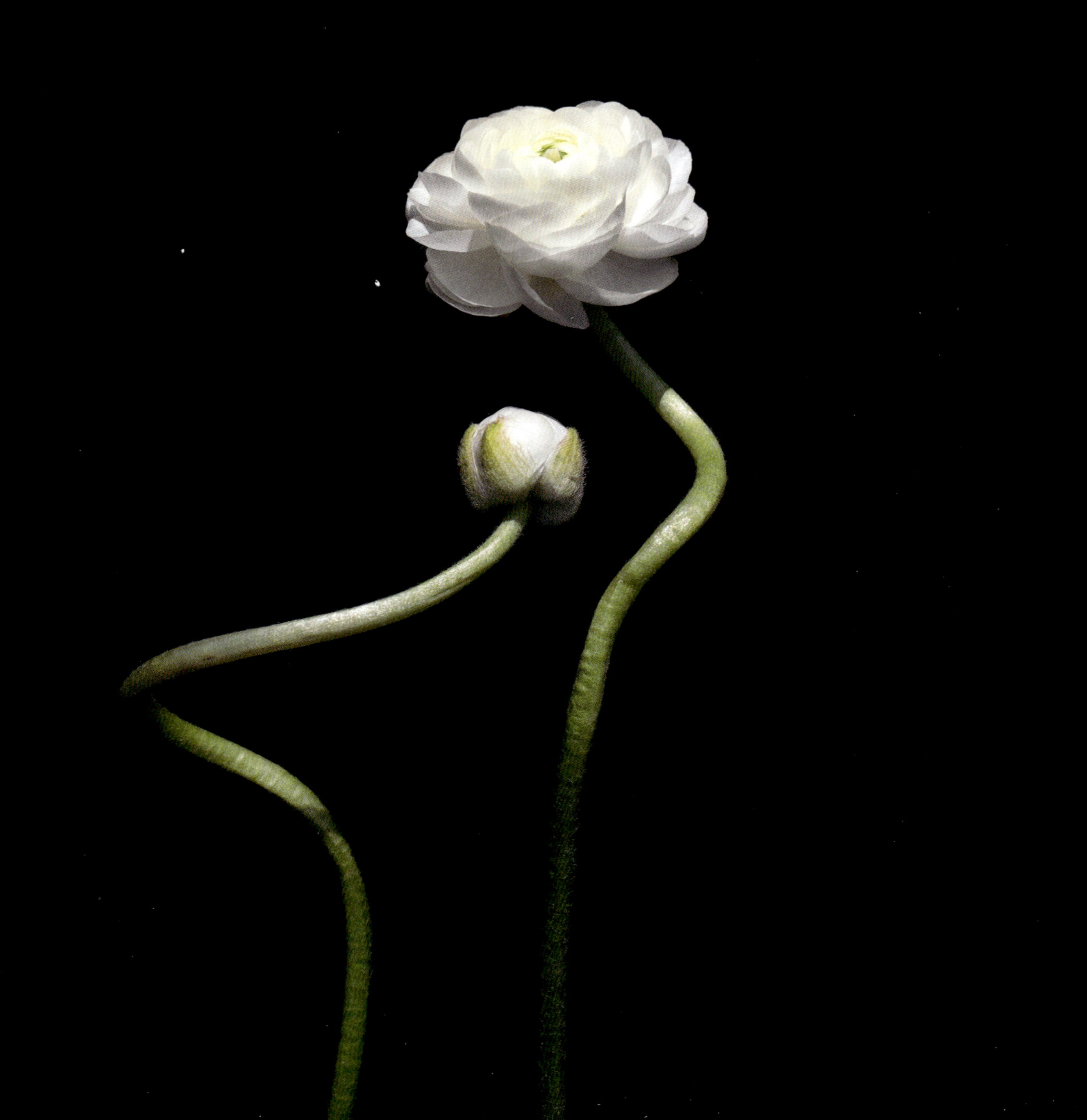

Acknowledgments

We are all connected. This became clearer as I contemplated how this book came into being. Without the love and support of so many, creating *Still Life* would have been impossible.

My heartfelt gratitude goes to my staunchest supporter and husband, Howard, who always believed in me. Every photograph between these two covers exists because of his abiding love. I am deeply indebted to my parents, grandparents, and the generations before them, whose love, resilience, and perseverance have shaped my life. To my wonderful children, Katie Alt Griffith, Drew Fulton Alt, and Valerie Lang Alt, thank you for your enduring love and support. Valerie and Saul Sutcher encouraged me to begin work on the book while we sheltered in place together during the Covid-19 pandemic. They generously cleared off their dining room table as they challenged me to "just begin." The ranunculus and peony blossoms featured in the book were gifts from my children and provided me with hours of inspiration.

The camera became my creative tool thanks to my beloved mentor Richard Olderman. We never solved all the mysteries of life, but the world became a much richer place for those of us who had the privilege of studying with him.

A sincere thank you to Peggy Brown, who suggested I participate in James Baraz's course, "Awakening Joy," which has provided me with invaluable tools for meeting the challenges of widowhood.

My deep appreciation goes to Deborah Gribbon and Jörg Colberg for their keen insights and expertise. My dear brother, Paul Fulton, offered his unwavering support and editing assistance. Many thanks to W. M. Hunt, my first collector and cherished friend, and to Alan Rapp, Cameron Wood, Constance Lewis, Belinda Bowling, Eileen Sutter, Amy Wilkins, and Takaaki Matsumoto for their invaluable input. Thank you to my community of friends and acquaintances, online and in person, for your ongoing encouragement. Your support made a world of difference in navigating the grief and giving me the courage to share my story.

I thank Laura Ekasetya, former director of the Lurie Garden in Chicago's Millennium Park, for the kind words she expressed to my children shortly after Howard's passing: "Tell your mother we will help her with the garden." The garden loomed large and felt like an impossible undertaking. Laura introduced me to Roy Diblik, Michael Ruminski, Kasey Eaves, Allison Sloan, and Christopher Fedak, whose collective knowledge and support ensured that the garden Howard began continues to thrive.

Finally, a heartfelt thank you to Douglas Tallamy, the prolific scientist who is responsible for inspiring a new generation of gardeners to respond to the urgency of replacing unproductive lawns with native gardens. He has created a roadmap to combat climate change, individually and collectively. Tallamy's book *Bringing Nature Home* was instrumental for Howard in reimagining our green space, which has, in turn, seeded many other native gardens.

Still Life: A Photographer's Journey through Grief and Gardening
by Jane Fulton Alt

First edition published in 2026 by MW Editions

MW Editions
New York City
www.mweditions.com
info@mweditions.com

Creative Direction and Designer: Takaaki Matsumoto, Matsumoto
Incorporated, New York
Editor: Amy Wilkins, Matsumoto Incorporated, New York
Production: Matsumoto Incorporated, New York

Printed and bound in Belgium

ISBN: 978-1-969303-00-5
Library of Congress Control Number: 2025921129

Distribution
D.A.P./Distributed Art Publishers, Inc.
75 Broad St., Suite 630
New York, NY 10004
www.artbook.com
orders@dapinc.com

Front cover: Persian buttercup (*Ranunculus asiaticus*), April 25, 2020 (detail)
Back cover: Common comfrey, Mexican sunflower, arborvitae, Chinese
clematis (*Symphytum officinale, Tithonia rotundifolia, Thuja occidentalis, Clematis
chinensis*), October 1, 2019

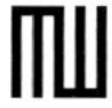

sian buttercup • Ranunculus asiaticus • tree peony • Paeonia suffruticosa
Faassen's catnip • Nepeta x faassenii • common lilac • Syringa vulgaris
garden tulip • Tulipa gesneriana • elderberries "Gerda" • Sambucus nigra
porphyrophylla "Gerda" • sugar maple • Acer saccharum • intermedia
wood fern • Dryopteris intermedia • Japanese painted fern • Anisocampium
japonicum • Chicago Hardy fig • Ficus carica "Chicago Hardy" • false
sunflower • Heliopsis helianthoides • blunt mountain mint • Pycnanthemum
muticum • Chinese silver grass • Miscanthus sinensis • cardinal flower
Lobelia cardinalis • gray-headed coneflower • Ratibida pinnata • August
lily • Hosta plantaginea var. "Grandiflora" • kiss-me-over-the-garden-
gate • Persicaria orientalis • blue cohosh • Caulophyllum thalictroides
oakleaf hydrangea • Hydrangea quercifolia • white coneflower • Echinacea
purpurea var. "Alba" • Mexican sunflower • Tithonia rotundifolia • cup
plant • Silphium perfoliatum • black-eyed Susan • Rudbeckia fulgida
swamp sunflower • Helianthus angustifolius • Lucky Charm Japanese
anemone • Anemone x hybrida "Lucky Charm" • garden speedwell
Veronica longifolia • borage • Borago officinalis • mountain fleece "Firetail"
Persicaria amplexicaulis "Firetail" • wild garlic • Allium vineale • Eastern
bottlebrush grass • Elymus hystrix • scarlet catchfly • Silene regia • Japanese
maple • Acer palmatum • hairy alumroot • Heuchera villosa • large-leaved
aster • Eurybia macrophylla • American basswood • Tilia americana
Maximilian sunflower • Helianthus maximiliani • Persian buttercup
Ranunculus asiaticus • tree peony • Paeonia suffruticosa • Faassen's catnip

...sneriana • elderberries "Gerda" • Sambucus nigra f. porphyrophylla "G...
...termedia • Japanese painted fern • Anisocampium niponicum • Chica...
...elianthoides • blunt mountain mint • Pycnanthemum muticum • Chine...
...ay-headed coneflower • Ratibida pinnata • August lily • Hosta plantagin...
...blue cohosh • Caulophyllum thalictroides • oakleaf hydrangea • Hydrange...
...nflower • Tithonia rotundifolia • cup plant • Silphium perfoliatum...
...ngustifolius • Lucky Charm Japanese anemone • Anemone x hybrida...
...ficinalis • mountain fleece "Firetail" • Persicaria amplexicaulis "Firetail...
...scarlet catchfly • Silene regia • Japanese maple • Acer palmatum • hair...
...merican basswood • Tilia americana • Maximilian sunflower • Helian...
...aeonia suffruticosa • Faassen's catnip • Nepeta x faassenii • common lilac...
...Sambucus nigra f. porphyrophylla "Gerda" • sugar maple • Acer saccharu...
...Anisocampium niponicum • Chicago Hardy fig • Ficus carica "Chicago...
...ycnanthemum muticum • Chinese silver grass • Miscanthus sinensis • car...
...August lily • Hosta plantaginea var. "Grandiflora" • kiss-me-over-the-g...
...oakleaf hydrangea • Hydrangea quercifolia • white coneflower • Echina...
...ant • Silphium perfoliatum • black-eyed Susan • Rudbeckia fulgida • swa...
...Anemone x hybrida "Lucky Charm" • garden speedwell • Veronica long...
...mplexicaulis "Firetail" • wild garlic • Allium vineale • Eastern bottlebru...
...cer palmatum • hairy alumroot • Heuchera villosa • large-leaved aster...
...nflower • Helianthus maximiliani • Persian buttercup • Ranunculus...
...assenii • common lilac • Syringa vulgaris • garden tulip • Tulipa gesner...
...gar maple • Acer saccharum • intermediate wood fern • Dryopteris inter...